SLEEPER TO LEADER

By

FAROOKH SENSEI

Disclaimer

This book draws from the author's personal experiences and research, aiming to provide educational and informational content. The author and publisher do not guarantee the accuracy or completeness of the information presented. The advice and strategies offered may not be suitable for every situation, and the author is not responsible for any loss or damage resulting from using this book.

Trademarks

All trademarks, service marks, product names, and company names or logos appearing in this book are the property of their respective owners. Including these trademarks does not imply any affiliation with, endorsement by, or approval of this book or its contents by the respective owners.

First Edition: **February 2025**

Printed in **India**

Table Of Contents

Sleeper To Leader

What does it take to rise from ordinary to extraordinary? To go from a passive observer to someone who leads with vision, purpose, and impact?

The answer isn't hidden in talent or privilege—it lies in the choices you make, the mindset you cultivate, and the actions you take daily. Leadership isn't just a title or a role; it's a journey of self-discovery and growth. It's about waking up to your full potential, breaking free from habits that hold you back, and stepping boldly into the person you're meant to be.

This book, *Sleeper to Leader*, is your roadmap to that transformation. Across 21 laws, you'll explore the traits, habits, and behaviours that separate those who merely dream from those who take action and lead. These aren't abstract theories—they're practical, relatable, and grounded in real-world examples that will inspire you to embrace change.

We'll begin with the Law of the Sleeper, which challenges you to recognise the patterns of stagnation and inaction that keep you stuck. From there, we'll confront habits like blaming others, overthinking, and procrastinating, which quietly erodes progress. Each chapter builds on the last, guiding you step by step through the mindset shifts and actions required to lead, not just in your career but in your family, relationships, and life.

Leadership is more than just breaking bad habits. In the second half of this journey, you'll learn to embody the traits of true leaders—whether it's taking calculated risks, embracing innovation, mentoring others, or creating a vision that inspires those around you. You'll discover the difference between a good leader who inspires trust and results and a great leader who leaves a legacy that changes lives.

This isn't just a book about leadership—it's a book about personal transformation. Whether you're an entrepreneur, a working professional, a family member, or someone navigating relationships, the principles in *Sleeper to Leader* apply to you. The tools you'll gain here will help you wake up to your potential and inspire others to do the same.

Are you ready to stop surviving and start thriving? Are you prepared to take responsibility for your growth, face your fears, and become the leader your life needs? If so, this is your moment. The journey from sleeper to leader begins now. Turn the page, and let's wake up the leader within you.

Farookh Sensei

Leadership MasterCoach
LEDGE International

LAW 1

The Law of the Sleepers

"The world moves fast; it doesn't wait, sleep too long, and it'll be too late." – Farookh Sensei

Sleepers

Have you ever seen a clock ticking but stuck at the wrong time? It moves but doesn't keep up with the world around it. That's what being a sleeper feels like—stuck in the illusion of progress while everything moves forward. On the surface, everything seems fine, but beneath it, you're disconnected from the changes and opportunities passing you by.

Being a sleeper isn't about laziness—it's about being unaware. It's holding onto routines, habits, or ways of thinking that no longer serve you. The challenge is realising it before the gap between where you are and where you want to be grows too wide. This chapter will help you wake up, reconnect, and move purposefully.

Example of Sleepers

Entrepreneur Perspective

Imagine you're running a family business that's been around for decades, built by your grandparents and passed down through the generations. It's something you're proud of—it's survived this long. But over time, you notice fewer customers, sales declining, and competitors taking a larger market share.

While the world moves forward, you're holding onto the same practices that worked a generation ago. You haven't updated your business model, explored digital tools, or noticed changing customer needs. You assume that because the business has always survived, it will continue to do so.

But deep down, you know something isn't right. You don't follow industry trends, haven't researched what your competitors are doing, and avoid learning new methods. You're a sleeper because you're stuck in tradition, disconnected from the changes around you. As the book *"What Got You Here Won't Get You There"* (by Marshell Goldsmith) teaches, past success is no guarantee of future survival without adaptation.

Professional Perspective

You've been working in the same role for years, using the same methods and tools you were taught when you first started. You're comfortable with how things are, confident that your experience is enough to keep you relevant. However, the workplace is evolving—new technologies, automation, and industry trends are reshaping work.

Colleagues around you are learning new skills, attending workshops, and adapting to these changes. On the contrary, you avoid learning because you think, *"I've been doing fine this way for years. Why change now?"* You don't read up on trends, don't attend training sessions, and ignore conversations about innovation.

You're a sleeper because you're out of touch with what's happening in your field. While others are growing and adapting, you're standing still, relying on outdated methods in a rapidly moving world. Just like in business, what worked before won't necessarily work tomorrow. Without updating yourself, you risk being left behind.

Family Perspective

You've always believed your family dynamic works well enough. Family traditions, habits, and routines have been passed down for generations and always seem to hold things together. But over time, you notice things have changed— family gatherings feel less meaningful, conversations are more superficial, and everyone seems busier and less engaged.

While the world around your family has evolved, you've stuck to the same ways of interacting. You don't talk about the challenges your kids face today, avoid discussing deeper emotions, and dismiss modern parenting techniques or new ways of communication. You assume that how your grandparents or parents managed relationships is still effective today.

Deep down, you sense that your family is drifting apart. You avoid learning to adapt to new challenges and miss opportunities to connect in ways that resonate with today's realities.

You're a sleeper because you've chosen to hold onto old patterns without noticing how much your family's needs have changed.

Husband-Wife Perspective

You've been in your relationship for years, and things have become predictable. You assume everything is okay because you've been together this long. You handle the daily responsibilities, share household tasks, and spend time together as usual. But over time, you notice the connection doesn't feel as strong—conversations have become surface-level, and moments of true intimacy or excitement are rare.

While the world around you and your relationship has changed, you've stayed in your comfort zone, assuming that what worked in the past will always work. You haven't explored new ways to communicate or adapted to changes in your partner's needs or interests. You don't read about improving relationships, avoid conversations about deeper feelings, and don't attempt to keep the spark alive because you believe, *"We're fine as we are."*

You're a sleeper because you're disconnected from the shifts in your relationship. By failing to notice and adapt to the evolving dynamics, you risk losing the deeper connection that brought you together in the first place.

Core Lessons

Awareness is the First Step Toward Change

You can't fix what you don't acknowledge. Recognising that you're stuck in old habits or outdated ways of thinking is the key to sparking transformation.

What Worked Yesterday Won't Always Work Tomorrow

Life evolves, and so must you. Success requires staying curious, learning new skills, and adapting to change instead of clinging to what's familiar.

Comfort Zones Are Silent Traps

Staying in your comfort zone may feel safe, but it prevents growth. To thrive, you must challenge yourself to step into the unknown and embrace the opportunities it brings.

Signs That You Are a Sleeper

In Business

You're relying on the same strategies and practices you've always used, even though sales are declining or competitors are pulling ahead. You avoid exploring new technologies or trends because they feel overwhelming.

At Work

You've been in the same role for years, using the same methods and tools, while others are learning new skills and growing in their careers. You avoid training sessions or new responsibilities, thinking, "I'm doing fine as I am."

In Your Family

Family traditions feel repetitive, and communication has become shallow. You avoid difficult conversations or adapting to your children's or partner's changing needs.

In Relationships

Your relationship feels like it's on autopilot. You rarely have deep conversations, avoid exploring new things together, and assume that time alone will strengthen the connection.

Practical Action Steps

Take a Hard Look at Your Reality

Ask yourself, "What's working in my life or business—and what isn't?" Write down areas where you feel stuck and reflect on how you got there.

Get Curious About What's Changing

Research trends in your industry, learn new skills or ask people around you for their perspectives. Stay informed and open to new ideas.

Challenge Your Comfort Zone

Commit to exploring one new thing this week—whether it's updating a system in your business, volunteering for a new task at work, or planning a different kind of family activity. Growth begins with small, intentional steps.

Seek Feedback from Trusted People

Ask colleagues, employees, family members, or your partner for honest feedback. Sometimes, others can see what you're missing.

Set Goals and Take Action

Identify one area in your life or work where you feel like a sleeper and set a small, actionable goal to change it. Don't wait for the "perfect time"—start now.

Being a sleeper doesn't mean you've failed; you've settled into habits that no longer serve you.

Awareness is the first step to waking up—recognise where you've been stagnant and where you need to grow.

The world is constantly changing, and to thrive, you must adapt, learn, and challenge your comfort zone.

By taking small, consistent actions, you can wake up from autopilot and create a life of growth and purpose. Wake up. The world is waiting for you.

LAW 2

The Law of the Blamers & Complainers

"The blamer points fingers, but nothing gets done; take control, and the battle is won." – Farookh Sensei

Blamers & Complainers

Imagine you're watching a soccer game, and every time the team loses, the coach blames the weather, the referee, or the other team's dirty tricks. At first, it might seem reasonable. But after a while, you realise the coach never looks at their strategies or players' performance. The team never improves because the focus is always on external factors, not what they can change.

In life, blame works the same way. When we point fingers at others or external circumstances, we protect ourselves from discomfort—but at the cost of progress. Blaming feels easier than reflecting, but it keeps us stuck. The key to growth is learning to own our role in every situation. This chapter is about breaking free from blame and stepping into responsibility, empowerment, and development.

Example of Blamers & Complainers

Entrepreneur Perspective

You've been running a business for years, but things haven't been going well lately. Sales are down, customers are complaining, and reviews aren't what they used to be. Each time something goes wrong, you have an explanation ready: *"It's the economy"* or *"Competitors are cutting prices and ruining the market."* When a customer gives negative feedback, you think, *"They're impossible to please."*

Your team struggles to address outdated processes or poor customer service issues, but you brush them off. You're convinced the challenge isn't internal—it's external. *"If the market weren't so challenging, everything would be fine,"* you tell yourself.

You're a blamer because you point fingers at everything but yourself. Instead of taking responsibility for what you can control—improving your services, updating your business model, or empowering your team—you focus on external factors. This mindset stops you from making the changes your business needs to thrive.

Professional Perspective

You've been in your role for a while but feel you're not succeeding. When a project doesn't go as planned, your first thought is, *"It's not my fault."* If you miss a deadline, you tell yourself, *"My boss didn't give me enough direction."* If a colleague performs better than you, you think, *"They must have had an easier task."*

You regularly complain about your workload, the office environment, and the lack of opportunities to advance. But when you reflect, you realise you haven't taken steps to improve your situation. You haven't asked your manager for feedback or explored new skills to make yourself stand out. Instead, you focus on what others are doing wrong or what the company isn't providing.

You're a blamer/complainer because you avoid owning your role in your setbacks. By shifting responsibility to others or external circumstances, you keep yourself stuck. Instead of finding ways to grow, you let excuses hold you back from progress.

Family Perspective

You've noticed tension growing in your family, especially between you and your kids. They seem distant, unmotivated, or defiant, and the atmosphere at home feels strained. Whenever there's conflict, your first instinct is to blame external factors: *"It's their school putting too much pressure on them,"* or *"Kids these days are glued to technology—it's ruining family connections."*

When your partner suggests ways to improve communication or spend more quality time together, you dismiss their ideas.

You think, *"If only the kids weren't so difficult, we wouldn't have these problems."* You're convinced that the issues aren't within your control—they result from outside influences or your children's behaviour.

You're a blamer because you avoid reflecting on how your actions or choices as a parent might contribute to the family dynamic. By shifting responsibility outward, you miss opportunities to connect more deeply with your family and foster a healthier environment at home.

Husband-Wife Relationship

Lately, the relationship feels strained, and you've been arguing more often. You think, *"If only they would listen more,"* or *"They're always so busy with work or their friends—that's why we're not connecting."* When there's tension, you point out what your spouse is doing wrong: *"You never help around the house,"* or *"You're always on your phone when I want to talk."*

When your spouse brings up their feelings, you deflect by saying, *"Well, if you didn't act like that, I wouldn't respond this way."* You believe the relationship would improve if they changed their behaviour. Still, you rarely reflect on how your actions might contribute to the problem.

You're a blamer because you focus on your partner's shortcomings instead of examining your role in the relationship's dynamics. By shifting responsibility to them,

you avoid addressing your behaviour and miss opportunities
to create deeper understanding and connection.

Core Lessons

Blame Is a Shield, but It Blocks Growth

When you blame others, you protect yourself from discomfort but miss opportunities to learn, grow, and improve.

Accountability Is the Foundation of Success

Taking responsibility for your actions, decisions, and outcomes puts you back in control and empowers you to create change.

Shifting from Blame to Solutions Changes Everything

Instead of focusing on whose fault it is, focus on what you can do to fix the problem. This mindset shift unlocks creativity, collaboration, and progress.

Signs You May Be a Blamer

In Business

You attribute failures to external factors like the economy, competitors, or employees. Instead of examining your strategies or leadership, you look for someone else to take the fall.

At Work

You point fingers at colleagues, managers, or company policies when things go wrong. You avoid reflecting on your role in mistakes or missed opportunities.

In Family

You blame family members for conflicts or problems, saying, "If they just listened to me, this wouldn't happen." You avoid considering how your communication or actions might contribute to the situation.

In Relationships

You blame your partner for misunderstandings or unhappiness. You think, "If they were more understanding, things would be better," without examining your behaviour or efforts to resolve issues.

Practical Action Steps

Pause Before You Point Fingers

The next time something goes wrong, pause and ask yourself, "What role did I play in this?" Shifting your focus to your actions will open the door to solutions.

Reframe the Situation

Instead of thinking, "Who's to blame?" ask, "What can I do to fix this?" This simple shift will move you from problem-focused to solution-focused thinking.

Seek Constructive Feedback

Ask trusted people for honest feedback about how you handle challenges. Hearing another perspective can help you see blind spots and areas for improvement.

Take Responsibility Publicly

When appropriate, acknowledge your role in mistakes—whether to your team, family, or partner. Taking ownership builds trust and shows leadership.

Turn Blame into Gratitude

When challenges arise, look for lessons instead of faults. For example, instead of blaming a failed project on external factors, focus on what the experience taught you and how you'll do better next time.

Key Takeaway

Blaming others feels easy at the moment but keeps you stuck in the same patterns.

Accountability is not about taking all the blame—it's about recognising your role and using that insight to grow.

Shifting your focus from blame to solutions empowers you to take control of your circumstances.

By taking responsibility for your life, you inspire trust, strengthen relationships, and create opportunities for meaningful growth.

Remember, letting go of blame is not about letting others off the hook—it's about stepping into the driver's seat of your own life.

LAW 3

The Law of the Doubters

"Doubt says no, but dreams say yes; take the chance, and you'll find success." – Farookh Sensei

Doubters

Imagine standing at the edge of a diving board, staring at the water. You've seen others jump, swim, and even enjoy the thrill of the dive, but your mind is racing. "What if I fall wrong? What if I embarrass myself? What if I'm just not good at this?"

This is how doubt works—it paralyses you, keeping you from leaping toward your potential. While everyone experiences doubt, the key is how you respond to it. Doubters stay frozen, letting their "what-ifs" and fears take control. But overcoming doubt allows you to step forward and discover what you're truly capable of. This chapter is about recognising the power doubt has over you—and learning to take action despite it.

Example of Doubters

Entrepreneur Perspective

You have an idea that could take your business to the next level—a new product, a different marketing strategy, or a bold expansion plan. But instead of acting, you hesitate. Thoughts like *"What if it doesn't work?"* or *"I'm not ready for this kind of risk"* dominate your mind.

You look at other entrepreneurs who have succeeded and think, *"They must have something I don't—more resources, more talent, or better luck."* You spend more time doubting yourself than strategising. Weeks turn into months, and that idea you once felt excited about stays shelved.

You're a doubter because your fear of failure and self-doubt prevent you from taking action. Instead of focusing on possibilities, you let uncertainty hold you back, keeping your business from reaching its full potential.

Professional Perspective

You've been offered a chance to lead a high-visibility project at work that could fast-track your career. But instead of being excited, you're overwhelmed by self-doubt. *"What if I mess up? What if I'm not good enough?"* you think.

You replay all the times you've made mistakes or didn't get recognition and convince yourself you're not ready. You politely decline the opportunity, telling your manager, *"I think someone else would be better for this."* As the project moves forward without you, you watch a colleague shine in the role you could have taken.

You're a doubter because your lack of confidence and fear of judgment keep you from stepping into opportunities for growth. Instead of believing in your abilities, you let doubt control your actions and stall your progress.

Family Perspective

You've been thinking about addressing an issue in your family—a miscommunication, a lack of quality time, or an unresolved conflict. But every time you consider bringing it up, doubt creeps in: *"What if it makes things worse?"* or *"What if they don't listen to me?"*

You convince yourself that staying silent and keeping the peace is better. You tell yourself, *"It's probably not as big of a deal as I think,"* even though the issue continues to bother you. Over time, the distance between family members grows, and the unresolved tension lingers.

You're a doubter because you let fear of confrontation and uncertainty stop you from addressing important family dynamics. Instead of trusting that you can handle the situation, you hold back, preventing growth and stronger connections.

Husband-Wife Perspective

You've noticed that your relationship feels less connected lately. You want to open up about your feelings or suggest ways to rekindle the spark, but doubt takes over. You think, *"What if they don't feel the same way?"* or *"What if they think I'm being too dramatic?"*

Each time you consider having the conversation, you convince yourself it's better to wait for the "right moment." Days, weeks, and months go by, and instead of addressing the distance, you stay quiet. You wonder if your partner notices the same things but feel too uncertain to ask.

You're a doubter because your fear of rejection or misunderstanding keeps you from communicating openly. By doubting your instincts and holding back, you miss the opportunity to strengthen your relationship and rebuild emotional intimacy.

Core Lessons

Doubt Is a Normal Part of Growth

Everyone experiences doubt when facing new challenges or opportunities. Growth and stagnation differ in how you respond to that doubt.

Your Strengths Outweigh Your Fears

Focusing on what you can do—and have already achieved—builds the confidence needed to silence self-doubt and take the next step.

Small Actions Defeat Big Doubts

The best way to overcome uncertainty is to start small. Each action chips away at fear and replaces it with confidence and momentum.

Signs Doubt Is Holding You Back

In Business

You hesitate to take risks, like launching a new product or entering a new market, because you fear failure or feel unprepared. You constantly second-guess your decisions, which delays progress.

At Work

You avoid volunteering for big projects or leadership opportunities because you doubt your abilities. You think, "What if I fail and everyone notices?" or "What if someone else is better for the role?"

In Family

You avoid making important decisions or initiating conversations about challenges, thinking, "What if I make the wrong call and things worsen?" You let indecision create distance or unresolved issues.

In Relationships

You hold back from expressing your feelings or taking steps to deepen your connection because you fear rejection or conflict. You think, "What if this makes things worse?" or "What if I'm not enough for them?"

Practical Action Steps

Identify the Root of Your Doubts

Ask yourself, "What am I afraid of? What's the worst that could happen?" Naming your fears often helps them feel less overwhelmed.

Focus on Your Strengths

Please write down your past successes and the skills or qualities that helped you achieve them. Remind yourself that you've overcome challenges before and can do it again.

Take One Small Step

Instead of waiting until you feel 100% ready, take the most minor action toward your goal. Even tiny wins can create significant momentum.

Challenge Your Negative Thoughts

When doubt says, "You can't," respond with evidence of why you can. Replace negative self-talk with affirmations like, "I'll figure it out" or "I'm capable of learning."

Surround Yourself with Support

Seek out mentors, friends, or colleagues who believe in you. Their encouragement can remind you of your potential and give you the push you need.

Key Takeaway

Doubt is natural, but it doesn't have to control you. Recognising its presence is the first step to overcoming it.

Focusing on your strengths and past achievements builds confidence and reduces the power of fear.

Taking even the most minor action can break the overthinking cycle and create growth momentum.

You don't have to eliminate doubt to move forward—acting despite doubt leads to success.

Doubt may never entirely disappear, but it's not your enemy—your invitation to grow. Your most significant potential lies just beyond your fear.

LAW 4

The Law of the Overthinkers

"Overthinking is like running on a treadmill—your mind works hard, but you never move forward." – Farookh Sensei

Overthinkers

Imagine you're sitting down to write an email, a seemingly simple task. But instead of typing, your mind spirals, "What if I phrase this wrong? What if they misunderstand me? What if this email ruins everything?" You rewrite it five times, double-check every word, and still hesitate to hit "send."

This is the trap of overthinking. It feels productive—like you're preparing for every possibility—but in reality, it's a cycle of doubt and indecision that keeps you stuck. Overthinking turns small decisions into mountains and drains your energy without delivering results. This chapter will help you recognise when your thoughts are holding you back and teach you how to break free from the paralysis of overthinking.

Example of Overthinkers

Entrepreneur Perspective

You've been brainstorming a new idea for months—a product launch, a new marketing strategy, or a potential expansion. But every time you think about taking the first step, your mind spirals, *"What if the market isn't ready? What if I mismanage the budget? What if I fail and ruin my reputation?"*

You spend hours researching, analysing, and tweaking your plans but never pull the trigger. You convince yourself you need more information, a better strategy, or perfect timing. Meanwhile, your competitors are making moves and gaining traction while your idea remains stuck.

You're an overthinker because your endless cycle of "what-ifs" prevents you from taking action. Instead of testing your ideas and learning through execution, you get caught in analysis paralysis, leaving your business stagnant.

Professional Perspective

You've been asked to lead a project or present an idea in a meeting, and at first, you feel excited. But as the deadline approaches, doubts and questions flood your mind: *"What if I miss an important detail? What if my boss doesn't like it? What if my colleagues think it's not good enough?"*

You revise your presentation repeatedly, agonising over every slide, word, and example. You stay up late tweaking details that may not even matter. When the day comes, you're so drained and anxious that your delivery feels forced, and you're unable to enjoy the opportunity.

You're an overthinker because your need for perfection and fear of making mistakes keep you trapped in a mental loop. Instead of focusing on progress and trusting your abilities, you overanalyse, undermining your performance.

Family Perspective

You've meant to plan a family trip or organise a family event. Still, every time you start, your mind goes into overdrive. *"What if everyone has scheduling conflicts? What if they don't enjoy it? What if it's too expensive?"* You figure out the perfect destination, timing, and activities but feel overwhelmed by all the possibilities.

Weeks pass, and you're still stuck debating the details. Family members ask what's happening, and you respond vaguely, saying you're "still figuring it out." Eventually, the opportunity passes, and the trip or event doesn't happen.

You're an overthinker because your obsession with making everything perfect prevents you from moving forward. By focusing on every possible outcome, you miss the chance to create meaningful moments with your family.

Husband-Wife Perspective

You've noticed tension in your relationship and want to discuss it with your partner. But instead of starting the conversation, you overthink every possible scenario *"What if they get defensive? What if I say the wrong thing? What if this turns into a fight?"*

You rehearse the conversation repeatedly, analysing every word and imagining every potential reaction. Days turn into weeks, and you still haven't said anything. You tell yourself, *"Maybe it's better to wait for the right moment,"* but the tension lingers, and nothing resolves.

You're an overthinker because you let fear of the unknown and a need for control keep you from communicating openly. By getting trapped in your thoughts, you avoid taking action and miss the opportunity to strengthen your relationship through honest dialogue.

Core Lessons

Overthinking Is an Obstacle Disguised as a Preparation

The more you dwell on possibilities and outcomes, the harder it becomes to take action. Actual progress comes from doing, not just thinking.

Perfectionism Fuels Overthinking

The need to get everything "just right" often leads to endless mental loops. Letting go of perfection opens the door to progress.

Clarity Comes from Action, Not Thinking

Taking even the most minor step forward brings more clarity than hours of overanalysing. Action creates momentum, which silences the noise in your mind.

Signs You're an Overthinker

In Business

You spend so much time analysing potential risks or outcomes that you delay decisions like launching a product, updating a strategy, or expanding your market. You fear making the "wrong move," so you make none.

At Work

You second-guess every choice, from how you structure a presentation to whether you should speak up in a meeting. You worry about every possible reaction and spend too much time perfecting minor details.

In Family

You overanalyse family decisions—vacation plans, parenting strategies, or even small purchases—thinking, "What if this upsets someone?" or "What if this backfires?" As a result, decisions are delayed or abandoned altogether.

In Relationships

You overthink your partner's words or actions, wondering, "What did they mean by that?" or "What if I say the wrong thing and they get upset?" This constant mental chatter creates unnecessary tension and prevents honest communication.

Practical Action Steps

Set a Time Limit for Decisions

Give yourself a specific amount of time to think about a decision, then commit to action. For example, "I'll spend 15 minutes thinking, and then I'll decide."

Ask, "What's the Worst That Could Happen?"

Often, the worst-case scenario isn't as bad as it seems in your head. Putting your fears into perspective can help you move forward.

Focus on One Thing at a Time

Overthinking thrives on juggling too many thoughts. Prioritise one decision or task and work on it step by step.

Take Imperfect Action

Accept that your first attempt doesn't have to be flawless. Progress matters more than perfection, so start small and adjust.

Write Down Your Thoughts

Journaling can help you untangle your mental loops. Once your thoughts are on paper, it's easier to see what's worth acting on and what's just noise.

Key Takeaways

Overthinking feels productive but leads to inaction. Taking even small steps forward is more valuable than endless mental debate.

Perfectionism often triggers overthinking. Letting go of the need for perfection allows you to focus on progress instead of possibilities.

Setting time limits, focusing on one thing at a time, and journaling are practical ways to quiet your mind and regain control.

Clarity doesn't come from thinking harder but from taking action and learning.

When you stop overthinking, you open the door to momentum, progress, and peace of mind. The time to act is now.

LAW 5

The Law of the

Procrastinators

"Procrastination builds a wall so tall; Climb it now, don't wait to fall." – Farookh Sensei

Procrastinators

Imagine you have an essential task due in a week, but instead of starting, you tell yourself, "I'll get to it tomorrow." Tomorrow comes, and suddenly, something else feels more urgent. You reassure yourself again, "I still have time." Before you know it, the deadline looms, and you're scrambling to get it done.

Procrastination is a cunning thief. It disguises itself as a harmless delay—just a little time to relax or think, but it costs you far more than you realise. It drains your energy, builds stress, and prevents you from achieving your full potential. This chapter will help you identify why you procrastinate, break the cycle, and reclaim your time and goals.

Example of Procrastinators

Entrepreneur Perspective

You've been meaning to update your business's website for months. You know it's outdated and that a refresh could attract more customers, but whenever you think about it, you tell yourself, *"I'll get to it when I have more time."* Weeks pass, and the "right time" never seems to arrive.

Instead, you fill your days with small, immediate tasks that feel productive but don't move your business forward. The big projects—creating a new product, improving customer engagement, or revisiting your business strategy—stay on your to-do list, untouched.

You're a procrastinator because you delay essential actions that could transform your business, convincing yourself that tomorrow will be better. Instead of addressing what matters, you focus on what's easy or urgent, leaving long-term growth on hold.

Professional Perspective

You've been assigned a major project with a deadline weeks away. At first, you feel confident, telling yourself, *"I have plenty of time to get this done."* But as the days go by, you keep putting it off. You tell yourself you'll start tomorrow, the next day, and the next.

When the deadline looms, you're in a frenzy—rushing to complete the project, skipping key details, and delivering something far from your best work. You regret not starting earlier, but you've convinced yourself you "work better under pressure."

You're a procrastinator because you avoid starting essential tasks until the last minute, relying on urgency to force you into action. Instead of using your time wisely, you delay and compromise the quality of your work.

Family Perspective

You've noticed that your family hasn't been spending much time together lately. You've meant to plan a game night, a weekend outing, or even a dinner where everyone puts their devices away. But whenever you think about it, you say, *"I'll organise it next week when things calm down."*

Weeks turn into months and nothing changes. You keep waiting for the "perfect moment" to make it happen, but life keeps getting in the way. Meanwhile, the family continues drifting apart, and you feel guilt for not taking action sooner.

You procrastinate because you delay meaningful efforts to strengthen your family relationships. By waiting for the right time, you miss opportunities to create lasting memories and improve connections.

Husband-Wife Perspective

You've been thinking about surprising your partner with a thoughtful gesture—a date night, a heartfelt note, or a meaningful conversation about how much you appreciate them. But every time the thought crosses your mind, you push it off, thinking, *"They'll understand I'm just busy right now—I'll do it later."*

Days turn into weeks, and the moment never comes. Meanwhile, the minor disconnects in your relationship start to grow, and your partner begins to feel unappreciated. You sense the tension but keep telling yourself, *"I'll address it when I have more time."*

You're a procrastinator because you delay taking simple but meaningful actions that could nurture your relationship. By postponing what matters, you risk letting minor issues grow into more significant problems and missing chances to deepen your connection.

Core Lessons

Procrastination Is Rooted in Avoidance

People procrastinate to avoid discomfort, whether fear of failure, perfectionism, or knowing where to start. Facing those fears head-on is the first step to overcoming them.

Action Builds Momentum

The hardest part of any task is starting. Once you take that first small step, the rest becomes more manageable, and momentum carries you forward.

Perfection Is the Enemy of Progress

Waiting for the "perfect time" or the "perfect plan" often leads to endless delays. Progress begins when you take action, even if it's imperfect.

Signs That You Are a Procrastinator

In Business

You delay launching new products, updating your website, or addressing problems, telling yourself, "I'll get to it when things calm down." Weeks pass, and nothing changes.

At Work

You put off starting projects until the last minute, telling yourself you "work better under pressure." While you may meet deadlines, the quality of your work or your stress levels suffer.

In Family

You avoid initiating family conversations or decisions, like planning vacations or resolving conflicts, because they feel overwhelming. You tell yourself, "We'll deal with it later."

In Relationships

You postpone meaningful conversations or gestures of love, thinking, "I'll do it when the time is right." Over time, your partner may feel neglected or unimportant.

Practical Action Steps

Break Tasks Into Smaller Steps

Big tasks feel overwhelming, so break them into manageable steps. Start with a tiny, simple action to build momentum.

Set Short Deadlines for Yourself

Give yourself a specific time frame to complete each step. For example, "I'll spend 30 minutes working on this today." Deadlines create urgency and focus.

Use the "2-Minute Rule"

If something takes less than two minutes to start, do it immediately. Often, starting is the hardest part, and this rule helps you overcome that hurdle.

Reward Yourself for Progress

Create small rewards for completing tasks—like taking a short break or enjoying a favourite snack. This reinforces positive behaviour and keeps you motivated.

Focus on the Benefits, Not the Task

Visualise how completing the task will feel and what it will achieve. This shifts your mindset from avoidance to motivation.

Key Takeaways

Procrastination is often about avoiding discomfort, but delaying action increases stress and reduces results.

Starting small creates momentum and helps you break the cycle of procrastination.

Breaking tasks into steps, setting short deadlines, and rewarding yourself can make even the most prominent tasks manageable.

Progress is more important than perfection. Don't wait for the perfect time—start now and adjust along the way.

Procrastination may feel like a temporary escape, but it steals your opportunities. Take control of your time, actions, and future today.

LAW 6

The Law of the Quitters

"Quitters stop when the road gets steep; Winners climb and reach the peak." – Farookh Sensei

Quitters

Imagine running a marathon. You're halfway through, your legs ache, and your lungs are burning. You see others around you slowing down, some even stepping off the course. You wonder, "Why am I doing this? Maybe I should quit, too."

Quitting is tempting, especially when things get tough. But while it feels like an escape at the moment, it's often a barrier between you and your potential. What separates those who succeed from those who stop is not talent or luck—persistence.

This chapter explores why people quit, how to recognise when you're on the verge of giving up, and what you can do to push through and achieve your goals.

Example of Quitters

Entrepreneur Perspective

You launched a business with enthusiasm and a big vision for success. But after a few months, things got tough. Sales didn't grow as quickly as you hoped, competitors seemed more substantial, and running the business was more complicated than you imagined.

Instead of pushing through and finding new strategies, you begin to lose motivation. You tell yourself, "Maybe this wasn't such a good idea," and start looking for an exit. You stop promoting your services, avoid tackling the challenges, and quietly let the business fade.

You're a quitter because you gave up when faced with obstacles. Instead of finding ways to adapt or improve, you walked away from the opportunity to learn and grow.

Professional Perspective

You started a new role at work and were excited to take on the challenges. But when things got difficult—complicated projects, harsh feedback, or unfamiliar responsibilities—you began to feel overwhelmed. Thoughts like "This is too much for me" or "I'm not cut out for this" crept in.

You stop trying as hard, avoid asking for help, and eventually start searching for a new job instead of addressing the challenges. When you leave, you tell yourself it's the company or the role that wasn't a good fit, but deep down, you know you gave up before you thoroughly explored.

You're a quitter because you let discomfort and self-doubt stop you from persevering. Instead of using the challenges to grow your skills and resilience, you walked away, missing the opportunity to push your limits.

Family Perspective

Your family has been going through a difficult time—misunderstandings, arguments, or unresolved conflicts. At first, you tried to work things out, but as the tension continued, you began to pull away emotionally. You tell yourself, "Nothing I say or do will make a difference," and stop trying to fix the relationships.

You retreat into your space instead of initiating conversations, seeking support, or connecting. Over time, the distance grows, and you find yourself avoiding family gatherings or meaningful interactions altogether.

You're a quitter because you gave up on repairing your family relationships. Instead of staying engaged and working through the challenges, you let frustration and doubt drive you away, leaving the bonds weaker than before.

Husband-Wife Perspective

In your relationship, you've noticed more conflicts and moments of frustration. At first, you tried to address the issues, but when progress didn't come as quickly as you hoped, you started pulling back. You think, "What's the point of trying if things will never change?"

You stop bringing up your concerns, stop making an effort to connect, and withdraw emotionally. When your partner tries to engage with you, you respond half-heartedly or avoid the discussion altogether. Over time, your relationship feels more distant, and you feel like giving up entirely.

You're a quitter because you let temporary challenges convince you to stop trying. Instead of trying to repair and strengthen the relationship, you allowed frustration to dictate your actions, leaving the connection weaker than it could be.

Core Lessons

Quitting Often Comes from Losing Your "Why"

When you forget why you started, challenges feel heavier, and motivation fades. Reconnecting with your purpose can reignite your drive.

Every Great Achievement Requires Endurance

Success isn't about avoiding difficulties—it's about persisting through them. Growth happens when you push beyond the urge to quit.

Small Steps Are Better Than Stopping

Even when progress feels slow, taking small steps forward is better than giving up entirely. Consistency beats quitting every time.

Signs That You Are a Quitter

In Business

You abandon ideas, projects, or strategies when you face challenges or don't see immediate results. You frequently think, "Maybe this just isn't for me."

At Work

You give up on complex tasks or avoid seeking promotions because you fear failure. You tell yourself, "It's easier to stay where I am."

In Family

You avoid resolving conflicts or taking on responsibilities because they feel overwhelming. You think, "Why bother? Things won't change."

In Relationships

You pull away when disagreements arise or when the spark fades. Instead of working to improve the relationship, you think, "Maybe this isn't worth it anymore."

Practical Action Steps

Reconnect with Your Why

Reflect on why you started in the first place. Write down your purpose or the goals you want to achieve and remind yourself of what's at stake.

Break Challenges into Smaller Pieces

If the path is overwhelming, focus on a tiny step at a time. Progress, no matter how small, builds momentum.

Reframe Setbacks as Lessons

Instead of seeing obstacles as reasons to stop, view them as opportunities to learn and grow. Ask yourself, "What can I take from this experience?"

Surround Yourself with Encouragement

Talk to supportive people who remind you of your potential and motivate you to keep going. Positive voices make a big difference when things get tough.

Celebrate Every Win

Acknowledge small victories along the way. Progress deserves recognition, and celebrating milestones keeps you motivated.

Key Takeaways

Quitting often stems from fear, frustration, or losing sight of your purpose. Reconnecting with your "why" is the key to regaining motivation.

Endurance is essential for success. Challenges are part of the journey, and pushing through them leads to growth.

Small steps forward are better than stopping. Even slow progress moves you closer to your goal.

Success belongs to those who don't give up. When the urge to quit strikes, remember why you started and take another step forward.

The journey may not be easy, but the reward is worth it. Don't stop now because you're closer to your goal than you think.

LAW 7

The Law of the Toxic Leaders

"Lead with force, and fear will grow; Lead with trust, and strength will show." – Farookh Sensei

Toxic Leaders

Leadership is a privilege, not a weapon. Imagine being part of a team where your ideas are dismissed, your efforts are undervalued, and fear replaces motivation. A toxic leader creates that environment—not by intention, but often by their unchecked behaviour.

The problem with toxic leadership is that while it may produce short-term results, it poisons the foundation of trust, morale, and long-term success. Toxic leaders micromanage, criticise without helping, and lead with ego rather than empathy. Their actions can destroy teams, relationships, and even their growth.

This chapter will help you recognise the traits of toxic leadership in yourself or others and teach you how to transition from a leader who controls to one who inspires.

Toxic leadership doesn't always involve shouting or micromanaging. It can be subtle, such as ignoring team feedback, taking credit for others' work, or creating an environment where people feel undervalued.

Toxic leaders often act out of insecurity, fear, or the need for control. While their actions may get short-term results, they harm morale, trust, and productivity in the long run.

Authentic leadership isn't about authority or ego—it's about creating an environment where others feel empowered, respected, and motivated. This chapter will help you identify toxic leadership tendencies, replace them with positive habits, and inspire your team to thrive.

Example of a Toxic Leader

Entrepreneur Perspective

You run a business and take pride in being in control. However, your leadership style involves micromanaging every detail, refusing to delegate, and criticising your team when things don't meet your expectations. When problems arise, you focus on blaming employees instead of looking for solutions.

Your team avoids giving feedback or presenting new ideas because they fear your harsh responses. Over time, morale declines, and productivity drops. You think, "They just don't care enough," but fail to recognise how your behaviour impacts their motivation.

You're a toxic leader because you create a hostile environment where fear and blame replace trust and collaboration. Instead of empowering your team, you undermine their confidence and stifle growth for them and your business.

Working Professional Perspective

You've been promoted to a managerial role and want to prove your value. However, you approach leadership with a heavy hand—demanding perfection, constantly pointing out mistakes, and rarely acknowledging your team's efforts. When deadlines are missed, or problems arise, you focus on assigning blame rather than working together to find solutions.

Your team begins to resent your approach. They don't feel supported or trusted, and communication becomes strained. You interpret their disengagement as laziness or incompetence, doubling down on your control and criticism.

You're a toxic leader because your actions foster negativity and resentment. Instead of creating a culture of collaboration and growth, you alienate your team and limit their ability to thrive under your leadership.

Family Perspective

You take on the role of decision-maker in your family, believing it's your responsibility to keep everything in order. However, your approach often involves controlling every aspect of family life—dictating schedules, making decisions without consulting others, and dismissing opinions that don't align with yours.

When family members express frustration, you interpret it as disrespect or ingratitude. You respond with harsh words, passive-aggressive comments, or even guilt trips, believing they don't understand how much you do for them. Over time, your family becomes distant and hesitant to communicate openly.

You're a toxic leader in your family because your need for control and lack of empathy create tension and disconnect. Instead of fostering mutual respect and collaboration, you inadvertently make your loved ones feel unheard and undervalued.

Husband-Wife Perspective

You often need to take charge in your relationship, assuming you know what's best. You make decisions for your partner without asking for their input, believing it's more efficient or that you're better at handling things. When disagreements arise, you dismiss their concerns or accuse them of being overly sensitive.

You frequently point out their flaws, framing them as "constructive criticism," but rarely acknowledge their strengths or contributions. Over time, your partner begins to withdraw, feeling unsupported and unappreciated.

You're a toxic leader in your relationship because your controlling and dismissive behaviour creates an imbalance of power. Instead of fostering a partnership built on trust and mutual respect, you undermine the connection by prioritising control over collaboration.

Core Lessons

Toxic Leadership Erodes Trust

A toxic leader focuses on control and criticism, which leads to disengagement and fear. Trust is the foundation of effective leadership; without it, teams and relationships crumble.

Empathy Is the Antidote to Toxicity

Great leaders understand their people, listen actively and lead with compassion. Empathy transforms leaders into role models who inspire and empower others.

A Toxic Environment Limits Growth

Toxic leadership creates a culture of survival rather than growth. Shifting to a positive, collaborative approach enables people to thrive and unlock their full potential.

Signs That You Are a Toxic Leader

In Business

You micromanage your team, rarely delegate, and criticise mistakes more often than praise accomplishments. You believe, "If I don't control everything, it'll fall apart."

At Work

As a manager, you focus more on finding faults than offering solutions. You rarely listen to your team's feedback and struggle to show appreciation for their efforts.

In Family

You dominate decisions, dismiss others' opinions, or use guilt to get your way. You believe, "I'm doing this for the family," but your actions make others feel undervalued or unheard.

In Relationships

You use criticism, sarcasm, or control to dominate conversations or decisions. Your partner may feel like they're walking on eggshells, unable to express their thoughts or feelings.

Practical Action Steps

Reflect on Your Behaviour

Ask yourself, "Do my actions build trust or create fear?" Be honest about how your leadership style impacts others and identify areas for improvement.

Listen More, Talk Less

Create opportunities for open communication. Ask your team, family, or partner for feedback, and truly listen without interrupting or defending yourself.

Focus on Empowerment

Delegate tasks and trust others to handle them. Offer guidance and support, but let people learn and grow through their experiences.

Acknowledge and Appreciate Efforts

Shift your focus from pointing out flaws to recognising achievements. Regularly express gratitude for others' contributions—it builds morale and trust.

Prioritise Empathy

Make an effort to understand others' perspectives. Ask questions like, "How can I support you?" or "What do you need from me to succeed?"

Key Takeaways

Toxic leadership stems from a focus on control, criticism, or ego, eroding trust, morale, and long-term success.

Empathy, active listening, and empowerment are key to becoming a leader who inspires rather than controls.

Reflecting on your behaviour and seeking feedback helps you identify and address toxic traits, creating a healthier environment.

Authentic leadership is measured not by how much power you have but by how much you empower others to thrive.

Leadership isn't about commanding—it's about connecting. Inspire trust, foster growth, and leave behind a legacy of positive change.

LAW 8

The Law of the Dreamers

"A dreamer who dares will touch the sky; One who waits will watch time fly." – Farookh Sensei

Dreamers

Close your eyes and imagine the life you've always wanted. The business you've dreamed of building, the career you've envisioned, the family you've hoped to nurture, or the relationship you've longed to strengthen. It's vivid, exciting, and full of potential.

Now, open your eyes. How close are you to making that dream a reality?

Dreamers are visionaries—they see possibilities that others often miss. But there's a trap: dreaming alone isn't enough. If you don't act on your dreams, they stay locked in your imagination, a constant "what if" that leaves you wondering why things never changed.

This chapter is about learning to honour your dreams by imagining them and making them a reality.

Example of a Dreamer

Entrepreneur Perspective

You have big ideas for your business—expanding into new markets, launching innovative products, and building a standout brand. You spend hours imagining what success will look like, envisioning accolades and financial freedom.

But when it comes to execution, nothing happens. You keep waiting for the "perfect time" or the "right conditions" to start. You tell yourself, "Once I have more money, experience, or a bigger team, I'll make it happen." Months pass, and while you continue to dream, your competitors are taking action and growing.

You're a dreamer because you focus on ideas without taking steps to turn them into reality. Your visions stay in your mind, disconnected from the actions needed to make them happen.

Working Professional Perspective

You often imagine yourself in a higher position at work—leading a team, earning recognition, and making an impact. You think about the skills you could develop or the initiatives you could lead, and you're sure you can do more.

But instead of taking action, you stay in your comfort zone. You tell yourself, "I'll go for that promotion once I'm ready," or "I just need a bit more time before I take the next step." You spend more time fantasising about what could be than preparing for it.

You're a dreamer because your ambitions remain ideas without follow-through. While you imagine a better future, your inaction keeps you stuck in the same role, far from the success you envision.

Family Perspective

You often think about ways to bring your family closer together—vacations, meaningful traditions, or heartfelt conversations that strengthen your bond. You can imagine family dinners filled with laughter and a home where everyone feels connected.

But those ideas stay in your head. You think, "We're all so busy right now. I'll plan something when life calms down." Days turn into weeks, and while you dream about what could be, the distance in your family relationships grows.

You're a dreamer because you focus on envisioning a close-knit family without taking concrete steps to create that reality. Your dreams remain just that—dreams—because you avoid turning them into action.

Husband-Wife Perspective

You often think about how excellent your relationship could be—spending quality time together, rekindling the romance, or communicating more openly. You imagine surprise dates, heartfelt conversations, and a stronger connection.

But instead of taking steps to make those moments happen, you wait for the "right time." You tell yourself, "Once work slows down, I'll plan something special," or "We'll talk about our feelings after things settle." Meanwhile, the day-to-day busyness takes over, and your relationship stays on autopilot.

You're a dreamer because you focus on what your relationship could become without taking action to nurture it. While your intentions are good, your inaction prevents your dreams from becoming reality.

Dreaming Without Action Leads to Frustration

Dreams are powerful but only inspire real change when paired with consistent action. Without effort, even the grandest visions fade into regret.

Your Dream Must Align with Your Purpose

The dreams that fuel your soul are the ones that connect with your values and passions. Pursuing them gives you the drive to push through challenges.

Small Actions Create Big Realities

Dreams often feel overwhelming because they seem so far away. Breaking them into small, achievable steps makes the journey manageable and the dream attainable.

Signs That You Are Only Dreaming

In Business

You constantly talk about where you want your business to go but take little action to get there. You create plans, but they stay on paper, and fear or hesitation keeps you from executing them.

At Work

You envision a promotion or career change but avoid taking steps to achieve it, like learning new skills, networking, or taking on more significant responsibilities.

In Family

You dream of building stronger relationships or creating memorable experiences but never follow through with concrete actions, like planning family activities or initiating essential conversations.

In Relationships

You imagine ways to improve your connection with your partner but don't communicate your feelings or take steps to make those dreams a reality.

Practical Action Steps

Define Your Dream Clearly

Write precisely what you want to achieve and why it matters. Be specific—vague dreams are more complex to act on.

Break It into Actionable Steps

Divide your dream into smaller, manageable goals. Focus on what you can do today, this week, or this month to move closer to your vision.

Take the First Step Now

Start immediately, even if it's something small. Send an email, research a course, or schedule a meeting. Action creates momentum.

Stay Accountable

Share your dream with a trusted friend, mentor, or partner. Let them hold you accountable and encourage you to stay consistent.

Celebrate Progress, Not Just Completion

Recognise and reward yourself for every milestone you achieve along the way. This keeps you motivated and focused.

Key Takeaways

Dreams are powerful, but they require action to become reality. Without effort, they remain distant possibilities.

Aligning your dreams with your purpose creates passion and resilience, helping you stay committed to your vision.

Small, consistent actions bridge where you are and where you want to be.

Taking the first step is always the hardest, but you'll build momentum and confidence once you start.

Dream boldly, but don't stop there. Take action, one step at a time, and transform your dreams into your imagined life.

LAW 9

The Law of the Learners

*"The one who learns will lead the way; The one who stops will
fade away." – Farookh Sensei*

Learners

Imagine a glass of water. Over time, it becomes stagnant if it's not refilled or flowing. Your mind works the same way. If you stop learning, your skills and knowledge become outdated, and your potential remains untapped.

Being a learner isn't just about taking courses or reading books—it's about staying curious, adapting to change, and embracing every opportunity to grow. The world is constantly evolving, and those who commit to learning thrive, while those who resist fall behind.

This chapter explores the mindset of a lifelong learner and how continuous learning can transform every area of your life.

Example of a Learner

Entrepreneur Perspective

You've always been curious about how to improve your business. You read books on entrepreneurship, attend workshops, and watch countless webinars on marketing, leadership, and scaling strategies. Your notebook contains ideas and insights; your laptop has bookmarked articles and saved resources.

But you rarely apply what you learn. You tell yourself, "I need to learn more before making big moves." You keep studying and gathering information but never take the next step to implement those lessons in your business. Your growth stalls because you're stuck in the learning cycle without action.

You're a learner because you love gaining knowledge. Still, your efforts fail to translate into tangible results unless you apply them.

Working Professional Perspective

At work, you're the one who's always signing up for training sessions, certifications, and online courses. You love learning new skills and understanding the latest trends in your industry. You've gained a wealth of knowledge, and your résumé looks impressive.

But when opportunities to use what you've learned arise—whether it's leading a project, pitching an idea, or solving a challenging problem—you hesitate. You think, "I'm still not ready," and convince yourself you need more experience or practice. While you keep learning, your colleagues are taking action and moving ahead.

You're a learner because you focus on acquiring skills but avoid stepping out of your comfort zone to put them into practice.

Family Perspective

You're passionate about improving your family relationships. You read parenting books, watch videos about communication strategies, and follow experts on social media for advice on strengthening bonds. You have many ideas for improving your family life—more quality time, improved communication, and deeper connections.

But when it's time to act on what you've learned—whether it's having a vulnerable conversation, implementing new routines, or changing old habits—you hesitate. You tell yourself, "It's not the right time," or "I need to read more to be sure this will work." Meanwhile, your relationships remain the same despite your good intentions.

You're a learner because you prioritise knowledge, but your efforts will not benefit your family relationships unless you take action.

Husband-Wife Perspective

You're eager to improve your relationship and often seek advice on strengthening it. You've read articles about effective communication, watched videos on keeping the spark alive, and even bookmarked couples' activities to try. You imagine how these strategies could bring you closer as a couple.

But when disagreements arise or life gets busy, you revert to old patterns. You think, "We'll try those ideas later," and postpone putting what you've learned into action. Your partner notices the gap between your intentions and actions, and the connection you want to build remains out of reach.

You're a learner because you absorb relationship advice. Still, you miss the opportunity to create meaningful change in your marriage without applying it.

Core Lessons

Learning Fuels Growth

Continuous learning is the key to personal and professional development. The more you learn, the more equipped you are to face challenges and seize opportunities.

Curiosity Is the Engine of Learning

The best learners are curious—they ask questions, explore new ideas, and stay open to perspectives that challenge their own.

Failure Is a Powerful Teacher

Mistakes and setbacks are opportunities to learn. Embracing them with a growth mindset turns failures into valuable lessons.

Signs That You've Stopped Learning

In Business

You rely on the strategies you've always used and avoid exploring new tools, trends, or techniques. You think, "What worked before will work again."

At Work

You don't take advantage of training opportunities or shy away from learning new skills because you already know enough.

In Family

You stick to traditional methods, dismissing the possibility that new parenting methods, communication techniques, or technologies could help your family thrive.

In Relationships

You assume you already understand your partner entirely and stop asking questions or exploring ways to grow together.

Practical Action Steps

Stay Curious

Make a habit of asking questions and seeking answers. Curiosity is the gateway to discovery and growth.

Set Learning Goals

Identify specific areas you want to improve—a skill, a habit, or a subject—and create a plan to learn about them step by step.

Learn from Failure

Reflect on mistakes and setbacks, asking yourself, "What can I learn from this?" Use those lessons to improve and adapt.

Expose Yourself to New Perspectives

Read books, attend seminars, or engage in conversations that challenge your thinking. Surrounding yourself with diverse ideas fosters growth.

Teach What You Learn

Sharing your knowledge with others deepens your understanding and reinforces what you've learned.

Key Takeaways

Learning is a lifelong process that keeps your mind sharp, your skills relevant, and your potential limitless.

Curiosity and a growth mindset are the foundation of becoming a valid learner.

Failure isn't a dead end—it's an opportunity to gain valuable lessons and grow stronger.

Commit to learning daily, and you'll continually adapt, thrive, and achieve your goals.

The most successful people aren't those who know everything—they're the ones who never stop learning. Stay curious, embrace challenges, and watch yourself grow beyond what you thought was possible.

LAW 10

The Law of the Strategists

"The wise don't rush; they set the stage. A strategist wins before the game's played." – Farookh Sensei

Strategists

Imagine trying to build a house without a blueprint. You might have all the materials and tools you need, but without a clear plan, every decision becomes guesswork, every mistake costs time and resources, and the final result is far from what you envisioned.

The same is true in life and work. Even the most fantastic ideas fall flat without a strategy to bring them to life. A strategist doesn't just set goals—they map out the steps to achieve them, anticipate obstacles, and adapt as needed. This chapter is about becoming the architect of your success by creating purposeful, actionable strategies that turn ideas into reality.

Example of a Strategist

Entrepreneur Perspective

As a business owner, you always consider the big picture. You create detailed business plans, outline step-by-step strategies, and set ambitious long-term goals. You also spend hours perfecting spreadsheets, researching market trends, and analysing competitor data.

But when it's time to execute, you hesitate. You tell yourself, "The plan isn't perfect yet," or "I need to refine it a bit more before taking action." You become so focused on strategy and preparation that you fail to implement the steps needed to bring your vision to life.

You're a strategist because you excel at creating plans, but without action, your strategies remain ideas instead of results.

Woking Professional Perspective

At work, you're known for your ability to think things through. When assigned a project, you're quick to draft a plan, define goals, and map out potential obstacles. You enjoy brainstorming sessions and crafting solutions, often impressing your colleagues with your foresight.

But when it comes to executing those strategies, you hesitate. You think, "What if I missed something?" or "Let me double-check everything before we move forward." Deadlines approach, and while you've spent most of your time planning, very little gets done.

You're a strategist because you prioritise creating detailed plans. Still, without timely execution, those strategies never deliver the impact they could.

Family Perspective

In your family, you're the one who likes to plan vacations, family projects, or even ways to strengthen bonds. You create schedules, outline budgets, and research activities to make everything run smoothly. You take pride in being prepared and having everything figured out beforehand.

But sometimes, focusing on the perfect plan leads to inaction. You tell yourself, "We'll go on that trip once everything is lined up perfectly," or "Let's wait until we can afford the best options." While refining your strategy, opportunities to connect and make memories pass you by.

You're a strategist because you value planning. Still, you miss chances to bring your ideas to life by prioritising perfection over action.

Husband-Wife Perspective

In your relationship, you're the one who's always thinking about how to improve things. You've talked about creating a financial plan, setting long-term goals as a couple, or scheduling more quality time together. You even outline actionable steps to make it happen—setting budgets, proposing calendars, or brainstorming date ideas.

But when it comes to implementing those plans, you stall. You worry that the timing isn't right or the plan needs more tweaking. You tell yourself, "We'll start when things calm down," but life keeps moving, and your strategies remain unused.

You're a strategist because you excel at planning ways to strengthen your relationship. Still, your hesitation to act keeps those plans from making a meaningful impact.

Core Lessons

Clarity Is the Foundation of Strategy

A strong strategy begins with a clear understanding of your goal. Without clarity, your actions lack focus, and your progress is scattered.

Flexibility Keeps Strategies Relevant

Even the best plans need adjustments. A great strategist is prepared to adapt when circumstances change, ensuring progress continues despite challenges.

Execution Is Where Strategy Comes to Life

A strategy on paper means nothing without action. Success comes from turning your plan into consistent, measurable steps forward.

Signs That You Lack Strategy

In Business

You set ambitious goals but don't outline how you'll achieve them. You jump between tasks without clear priorities or rely on trial and error to find solutions.

At Work

You feel like you're always busy but rarely make meaningful progress. You tackle tasks reactively without planning how they connect to your long-term goals.

In Family

You have goals like saving for vacations, improving communication, or creating traditions, but no clear steps to achieve them. You try things sporadically but lack a consistent approach.

In Relationships

You know you want to strengthen your bond with your partner. Still, you don't take the time to plan meaningful conversations, activities, or efforts to grow together.

Practical Action Steps

Define Your Goal Clearly

Ask yourself, what exactly do I want to achieve, and why does it matter? Write your goal in specific, measurable terms so you can track progress.

Break It Down

Divide your goal into smaller, actionable steps. For example, if your goal is to grow your business, break it into tasks like improving marketing, building partnerships, or refining your product.

Prioritise Your Actions

Not everything needs to be done at once. Focus on the tasks that will have the most significant impact first. Use tools like to-do lists or project management apps to stay organised.

Anticipate Challenges

Think ahead about what might go wrong and how you'll handle it. This preparation keeps you from being derailed when obstacles arise.

Track and Adjust

Review your progress regularly. Don't be afraid to tweak your strategy if something isn't working. Flexibility ensures your plan stays effective.

Key Takeaways

Every great strategy starts with a clear goal. Without it, actions lack purpose and focus.

Strategy isn't static—it's a living process that evolves as circumstances change. Stay adaptable to remain effective.

Execution is the most essential part of any strategy. Success requires consistent, focused action toward your goals.

A strategist plans for progress, anticipates obstacles, and adapts to ensure long-term success.

Being a strategist means taking control of your future with purpose and precision. With a clear plan and consistent action, no goal is out of reach.

LAW 11

The Law of the Innovators

"The world won't change with thoughts so old; An innovator dares to break the mold." – Farookh Sensei

Innovators

Imagine walking through a forest. Most people stick to the trail, following the path others have already carved. But an innovator looks at the untouched spaces, thinking, "What if I take a different route? What could I discover?"

Innovation is about breaking free from "how things have always been done" and daring to ask, "How can this be better?" It's not just for inventors or tech geniuses—for anyone willing to challenge the status quo, whether in business, work, family, or personal growth.

This chapter will help you unlock an innovator's mindset, embrace creativity, and turn bold ideas into reality.

Example of an Innovator

Entrepreneur Perspective

As a business owner, you're full of ideas—creative solutions, unique products, or groundbreaking strategies that could set your company apart. You love brainstorming and envisioning ways to revolutionise your industry.

But when it's time to act, you hesitate. You think, "What if the idea fails? What if my customers don't respond well? What if I waste money on this?" You keep your ideas in your head or on paper, telling yourself you'll pursue them later when the time feels right. Meanwhile, your competitors take risks, launch new products, and capture market share.

You're an innovator because you excel at creating creative ideas. Still, your fear of failure or reluctance to act prevents those ideas from becoming reality.

Working Professional Perspective

At work, you're the person who's always coming up with ways to improve processes, enhance productivity, or solve long-standing problems. You enjoy thinking outside the box and imagining how things could be better.

But you hold back when pitching your ideas to leadership or implementing them. You worry about rejection, criticism, or being seen as unrealistic. You tell yourself, "This might not be the right time," your innovative ideas remain unused. In contrast, others stick to the same outdated practices.

You're an innovator because you thrive on creativity and fresh ideas. Still, without action or confidence to share them, your potential for impact is wasted.

Family Perspective

In your family, you're always thinking of new ways to make life more enjoyable and meaningful—fun traditions, creative ways to spend time together, or unique solutions to everyday challenges. You love imagining what could make your family closer or happier.

However, you rarely share or act on your ideas. You think, "What if they don't like it?" or "It's probably not worth the effort right now." So, instead of bringing fresh energy to your family, you stick to the usual routines, letting opportunities for creativity slip away.

You're an innovator because you dream up fantastic ideas for your family. Still, your reluctance to act keeps those ideas from bringing joy or strengthening your bonds.

Husband-Wife Perspective

In your relationship, you're constantly coming up with ideas to keep things exciting—a surprise date, a heartfelt gift, or even ways to improve communication. You think about how to rekindle the spark or make your partner feel special, and your creativity excites you.

But you hesitate when it's time to implement those ideas. You think, "What if they think it's silly?" or "What if I get it wrong?" So, you keep your ideas to yourself, and your relationship continues in its usual rhythm without the energy or excitement you imagined.

You're an innovator because you have creative visions for your relationship. Still, your fear of judgment or failure keeps those ideas from enriching your connection.

Core Lessons

Innovation Starts with Curiosity

Innovators ask questions, challenge assumptions, and explore possibilities. Curiosity fuels the discovery of better ways to do things.

Failure Is Part of the Process

Great ideas rarely succeed on the first try. Innovators see failure as feedback and use it to refine their ideas rather than abandoning them.

Collaboration Sparks Innovation

Innovation thrives in diverse environments where ideas are shared, combined, and challenged. Working with others broadens perspectives and leads to breakthroughs.

Signs That You Are Not Innovating

In Business

You stick to the same products, services, or strategies year after year, even when results stagnate. You avoid experimenting because you're afraid of wasting resources or failing.

At Work

You follow the same routines and processes without questioning whether there's a better way. You avoid sharing ideas in meetings because you fear they'll be rejected.

In Family

Your family activities, communication styles, and routines feel repetitive and uninspired. You resist trying new traditions or approaches, thinking, "This is how we've always done it."

In Relationships

You've fallen into a predictable pattern with your partner, avoiding creative ways to connect or solve problems. You hesitate to suggest new ideas, fearing they might not work.

Practical Action Steps

Start Asking "What If?"

Look at your work, business, or relationships and ask, "What if we tried something different? What if this could be improved?" Let curiosity guide your thinking.

Experiment with Small Changes

Innovation doesn't require drastic overhauls. Start by tweaking one process, trying a new activity, or brainstorming ways to improve something small.

Seek Inspiration from Outside Sources

Read books, watch videos, or attend events that expose you to new ideas. Learn from innovators in other fields and adapt their concepts to your own.

Collaborate and Brainstorm with Others

Surround yourself with diverse thinkers who can challenge your ideas and offer new perspectives. Collaboration often leads to creative breakthroughs.

Celebrate and Learn from Failures

When something doesn't work, don't see it as the end—see it as a step forward. Ask, "What did I learn from this, and how can I improve?"

Key Takeaways

Innovation starts with curiosity and the willingness to question "how it's always been done."

Failure isn't a dead end—it's a step toward discovery. Innovators learn, adapt, and keep going.

Collaboration with diverse perspectives often leads to breakthroughs that wouldn't happen alone.

Small experiments can lead to significant changes. Innovation is about progress, not perfection.

Be bold. Think differently. The world doesn't just need followers—it needs innovators willing to pave new paths for themselves and others.

LAW 12

The Law of the Risk Takers

*"Play it safe and stay the same, Or take the risk and change the
game." – Farookh Sensei*

Risk Takers

Imagine standing at the edge of a cliff overlooking a deep, beautiful valley. Below lies everything you've ever wanted: success, growth, and fulfilment. To get there, you have to take a leap. But fear holds you back. "What if I fall? What if I fail?"

Risk-taking feels scary because it challenges your instinct to stay safe. But without taking risks, you miss opportunities to grow, learn, and achieve greatness. This chapter will show you why calculated risks are essential, how to embrace uncertainty, and how stepping outside your comfort zone can transform your life.

Example of a Risk Taker

Entrepreneur Perspective

You've been running your business for a while and see an opportunity to expand—maybe launching a new product, entering a new market, or scaling operations. It could take your business to the next level but involves uncertainty. It will require financial investment, time, and stepping into unfamiliar territory.

Instead of taking a leap, you hesitate. You think, "What if I fail and lose everything?" or "What if this doesn't work out?" You decide to stick to what's safe, focusing on maintaining the status quo rather than pursuing growth. Months pass, and while competitors are growing, your business remains stagnant.

You're not a risk taker because fearing failure keeps you from exploring opportunities that could transform your business. By avoiding uncertainty, you limit your potential for innovation and success.

Working Professional Perspective

You've been offered a new role at work, one that comes with more responsibility and visibility. It's a great opportunity and a challenge that feels outside your comfort zone. You begin to worry, "What if I mess up? What if I'm not good enough?"

Instead of taking the promotion, you decline, telling yourself, "I'm not ready yet." You stick to your current role, where you feel safe and capable, even though it no longer challenges you. Months later, you watch a colleague excel in the role you turned down and wonder what might have been.

You're not a risk taker because your fear of stepping outside your comfort zone stops you from pursuing growth. By avoiding challenges, you miss opportunities to advance in your career.

Family Perspective

Your family has been in a routine for years. You've thought about making a significant change—moving to a new city, starting a new tradition, or introducing a lifestyle change that could improve everyone's well-being. You know it could be a positive step, but it feels risky.

You start second-guessing, "What if it's the wrong move? What if it disrupts the family too much?" Instead of taking action, you convince yourself to stay where it's safe and familiar, even though you know things could be better.

You're not a risk taker because your fear of disrupting the status quo keeps you from pursuing meaningful changes that could benefit your family. By avoiding risk, you limit the potential for growth and connection.

Husband-Wife Perspective

In your relationship, there's a sensitive topic you've been avoiding—something that's been weighing on you for a while. You want to bring it up and have an honest conversation, but you're worried about how your partner might react. "What if it causes an argument?" you think.

You keep your feelings to yourself instead of taking risks and opening up. The issue remains unresolved, and the distance between you and your partner slowly grows. You stay in the comfort of silence, even though it prevents you from addressing the root of the problem.

You're not a risk taker because your fear of conflict or vulnerability stops you from having difficult but necessary conversations. By avoiding risks in communication, you miss the chance to strengthen trust and deepen your connection.

Core Lessons

Risk Is the Bridge Between Potential and Achievement

Every significant accomplishment requires taking risks, whether starting a business, seeking a promotion, or pursuing a dream. Without risks, growth stalls.

Calculated Risks Are the Key to Success

Risk-taking isn't about recklessness—it's about weighing the potential rewards against the downsides and confidently taking action.

Fear Is a Compass for Growth

The things you're most afraid of often point to the areas where you have the most room to grow. Facing those fears unlocks your true potential.

Signs That You Avoid Taking Risks

In Business

You hesitate to launch new products, expand into new markets, or try different strategies because you're afraid of failure or losing what you've built.

At Work

You stay in your comfort zone, avoiding challenges like applying for promotions, leading projects, or pitching new ideas because you fear rejection or criticism.

In Family

You avoid making big decisions—like moving to a new city, changing family routines, or addressing conflicts—because you don't want to disrupt the status quo.

In Relationships

You resist opening up emotionally, having difficult conversations, or trying new ways to connect because you're afraid of vulnerability or failure.

Practical Action Steps

Start with Small Risks

Build your risk-taking muscles by starting small. Say yes to a new opportunity, share an idea in a meeting, or try something new in your daily routine.

Weigh the Risks and Rewards

Ask yourself, "What's the worst that could happen, and what's the best possible outcome?" If the rewards outweigh the risks, take the leap.

Learn to Reframe Fear

Instead of seeing fear as a signal to stop, see it as a sign that you're about to grow. When you feel nervous, remind yourself, "This is where change happens."

Surround Yourself with Bold Thinkers

Spend time with people who take risks and embrace challenges. Their mindset and energy will inspire you to do the same.

Focus on the Long-Term Benefits

Remember that taking risks, even when they don't work out, leads to growth, learning, and resilience. Look at the bigger picture.

Key Takeaways

Risk-taking is essential for growth and success. Without it, you remain stuck in your comfort zone, missing opportunities for transformation.

Calculated risks, weighing potential rewards against possible downsides, are the foundation of wise decision-making.

Fear isn't your enemy—it's a guide that points you toward areas where you can grow and evolve.

Start small, surround yourself with bold thinkers, and take one step at a time toward more significant, braver decisions.

Your most outstanding achievements lie just beyond your comfort zone. Dare to take the leap.

LAW 13

The Law of the Starters

"If you don't start, you'll never know; A single step can make you grow." – Farookh Sensei

Starters

Imagine staring at a blank canvas, a new project, or a big idea. You know what you want to create or accomplish, but instead of starting, you hesitate. You think, "What if I fail? What if it's not good enough? What if I don't know what I'm doing?"

The truth is, starting is the hardest part of any journey. It's where fear, self-doubt, and procrastination all try to hold you back. But without starting, you'll never know what you can achieve. This chapter is about overcoming that first hurdle, embracing the courage to begin, and creating the momentum to turn your ideas into reality.

Example of a Starter

Entrepreneur Perspective

You've been sitting on a business idea for months, maybe years. You've done the research, drafted a rough business plan, and envisioned what success could look like. You know your idea has potential, but doubts creep in every time you consider launching "What if I fail?" or "What if it's not the right time?" You keep telling yourself, "I'll start once I have more resources," or "I need to plan this out a bit more before I take the first step." Weeks turn into months, and while the dream remains alive in your mind, you never take the leap to bring it into reality.

You're not a starter because your hesitation to take the first step keeps you stuck in the idea phase. Without action, even the best business ideas stay unrealised.

Working Professional Perspective

You've been considering taking on a new challenge at work—maybe leading a project, proposing an idea, or pursuing a certification to advance your career. You've thought it through and even started researching the steps you'd need to take, but you keep hesitating.

You tell yourself, "I'll wait until my workload lightens up," or "What if I don't do it perfectly?" As the days pass, you notice others stepping into new opportunities and gaining recognition. At the same time, you stay in your usual routine.

You're not a starter because your reluctance to take the first step stops you from moving forward in your career. By delaying action, you miss chances to grow and show your potential.

Family Perspective

You've been thinking about ways to bring your family closer— maybe planning a family game night, organising a trip, or starting a new tradition. You're excited about the possibilities but hesitate to begin. You think, "What if no one participates?" or "What if it doesn't go as planned?"

You keep putting it off, waiting for the "perfect time," but the right moment never seems to come. Meanwhile, the distance in your family relationships continues to grow, and the opportunities for connection slip away.

You're not a starter because your hesitation to take action prevents you from creating meaningful experiences with your family. Without starting, even the best intentions remain just ideas.

Husband-Wife Perspective

You've wanted to improve your relationship with your partner—maybe by having more date nights, communicating more openly, or addressing minor conflicts before they grow.

You've thought about what you could do and even talked about it in passing, but you haven't taken the first step.

You keep telling yourself, "We'll start when things settle down," or "What if it feels awkward at first?" Days turn into weeks, and the effort you want to make stays on hold while the relationship continues on autopilot.

You're not a starter because your reluctance to initiate action keeps your relationship in the same pattern. Without starting, the changes you hope for never have a chance to take root.

Core Lessons

Starting Creates Momentum

The first step is always the hardest, but once you take it, the energy of progress makes the next steps easier. Starting is the spark that ignites action.

Perfection Isn't Required to Begin

Waiting for the perfect plan or time often leads to endless delays. Progress begins when you start, even if it's messy or imperfect.

Action Defeats Fear

Fear thrives in inaction. When you start, even with small steps, fear begins to fade, replaced by confidence and clarity.

Signs That You Struggle to Start

In Business

You have ideas for new ventures, products, or strategies but never take the first step to bring them to life. You spend more time planning than acting.

At Work

You hesitate to volunteer for new projects, delaying your chance to learn or grow because you think, "What if I'm not ready?"

In Family

You avoid initiating meaningful family conversations, projects, or activities because you're unsure where to begin or fear things won't go as planned.

In Relationships

You put off making changes or expressing your feelings, telling yourself, "I'll talk about it later," but later never comes.

Practical Action Steps

Define the First Step

Break your goal into the most minor possible actions you can take now. For example, if you're starting a new business, the first step could be researching your target audience.

Set a Start Deadline

Commit to a specific date and time to begin. Don't leave it open-ended—decide, "I'll start tomorrow at 10 AM," and hold yourself to it.

Embrace Imperfection

Remember that starting doesn't mean you need to have everything figured out. Progress is more important than perfection.

Tell Someone Your Plan

Share your intention to start with a friend, mentor, or partner. Their encouragement and accountability can push you to take that first step.

Reward Yourself for Starting

Celebrate the act of beginning, no matter how small the step. Recognise that starting is a victory in itself.

Key Takeaways

Starting is often the most challenging part of any journey but also the most crucial. Without action, your ideas remain dreams.

Perfection is not required to begin. Starting messy or uncertain is better than not starting at all.

Taking the first step creates momentum, making the next steps more straightforward and natural.

Define your first action, set a start date, and celebrate the courage it takes to begin.

Every outstanding achievement begins with a single step. Take that step today, and watch how quickly your momentum grows.

LAW 14(A)

The Law of the Safe Players

"A safe player watches, afraid to leap; While leaders rise and climb the steep." – Farookh Sensei

Safe Players

Imagine you're in a soccer game and pass it to someone else every time you get the ball. You never take the shot, even when you have a clear opportunity. You tell yourself it's safer to let others take the risk because you don't want to miss or make a mistake.

This is how safe players operate in life. They avoid risks, stick to what's comfortable, and focus on staying secure. While this might seem wise, it often leads to missed opportunities and stagnation. Playing it safe feels cozy, but it can also mean watching others grow, succeed, and win while you remain stuck in the same place.

This chapter will help you recognise the cost of always playing it safe and encourage you to step out of your comfort zone to embrace growth.

Example of a Safe Player

Entrepreneur Perspective

You've been running a steady business, sticking to what's familiar and proven. Your products or services are reliable and have a loyal customer base. But deep down, you know you're playing it safe.

You avoid launching bold ideas or entering new markets because you think, "What if it doesn't work? I can't afford to lose what I've built." Instead of taking risks that could lead to significant growth, you focus on maintaining the status quo. Meanwhile, competitors willing to take risks start gaining ground and capturing opportunities you passed up.

You're a safe player because your fear of uncertainty keeps you from exploring possibilities that could elevate your business. By avoiding risks, you miss out on innovation and long-term success.

Working Professional Perspective

You stick to your assigned tasks at work and avoid taking on challenges that might stretch you. You're reliable and consistent, but you shy away from anything that feels risky— like leading a project, presenting an idea, or pursuing a promotion.

You think, "What if I make a mistake?" or "What if I'm not good enough?" So, you stay in your comfort zone, focusing on tasks you've already mastered. While others step up and take risks, earning recognition and advancement, you stay where it feels safe.

You're a safe player because fearing failure or judgment keeps you from reaching for more significant opportunities. By avoiding challenges, you limit your growth and potential.

Family Perspective

You avoid addressing complex topics or making significant changes in your family because you don't want to disrupt the peace. Whether it's a disagreement that needs resolution, a new family routine, or a big decision like moving or taking a trip, you stick to what's comfortable and predictable.

You think, "What if it causes conflict?" or "What if it doesn't work out?" So, instead of exploring opportunities to improve family relationships or dynamics, you let things stay as they are, even if they're not ideal.

You're a safe player because your fear of rocking the boat keeps you from taking action that could bring your family closer or create positive change.

Husband-Wife Perspective

In your relationship, you avoid having tough conversations or trying new ways to connect because you fear the outcome. Whether it's expressing a need, discussing unresolved issues, or planning something adventurous, you hold back, thinking, "What if this creates tension?" or "What if it doesn't go well?"

You stick to familiar routines and avoid taking emotional risks, even when you know your relationship could benefit from deeper communication or more excitement. Over time, this safety-first approach leaves your relationship feeling stagnant and predictable.

You're a safe player because your reluctance to take emotional or relational risks prevents growth and deeper intimacy. By avoiding discomfort, you miss opportunities to strengthen your bond.

Safety Limits Growth

Sticking to what's familiar keeps you from exploring new opportunities or realising your full potential. Growth requires discomfort.

Calculated Risks Are Essential for Success

Being bold doesn't mean being reckless. Taking calculated risks allows you to move forward without unnecessary fear.

Fear Is a Companion, Not a Stop Sign

Playing it safe often comes from fear. Learning to act despite fear separates those who grow from those who stay stagnant.

Signs That You're a Safe Player

In Business

You stick to tried-and-true methods, avoiding new strategies or markets because you fear failure. You hesitate to invest in innovation or expand because it feels too risky.

At Work

You avoid volunteering for challenging projects, thinking, "What if I mess up?" or "What if someone else is better at this?" You stay in your comfort zone, focusing on tasks you've mastered.

In Family

You resist changes in family routines, traditions, or decisions, preferring to stick to what's worked in the past. Avoid addressing deeper family issues because leaving things as they are feels safer.

In Relationships

You avoid initiating meaningful or vulnerable conversations because you fear conflict or rejection. You stick to routine interactions, even if they feel unfulfilling, because they're comfortable.

Practical Action Steps

Identify What You're Avoiding

Reflect on the areas in your life where you're sticking to comfort. Ask yourself, "What am I afraid of? What's holding me back?"

Take a Small Risk This Week

Start with something manageable. For example, share a bold idea in a meeting, try a new activity with your family, or bring up a meaningful topic with your partner.

Reframe Failure as Learning

Instead of seeing failure as the worst outcome, view it as an opportunity to grow. Ask yourself, "What can I learn if this doesn't go as planned?"

Surround Yourself with Bold Thinkers

Spend time with people who take risks and challenge themselves. Their mindset and energy can inspire you to do the same.

Visualise Success

Picture what could happen if you step out of your comfort zone and succeed. Let that vision motivate you to take action.

Key Takeaways

Playing it safe may feel secure, but it keeps you from growing, achieving, and reaching your full potential.

Growth requires stepping out of your comfort zone and taking calculated risks.

Failure is not the enemy—staying stuck in safety is. Every risk teaches you something valuable.

Start small, embrace discomfort, and take bold steps toward the life and success you truly want.

The game of life isn't won by those who never take a shot. It's time to step out of the shadows, take a chance, and watch yourself grow.

LAW 14(B)

The Law of the Solo Players

"A solo player may stand so tall; But one alone can't win it all."
– Farookh Sensei

Solo Players

Imagine you're building a house but insist on doing everything yourself—laying bricks, wiring electricity, painting walls, and even designing the furniture. The progress is slow, mistakes pile up, and before long, exhaustion sets in. What could have been a beautiful, finished home becomes a half-built structure that never reaches its full potential.

That's the trap of the solo player. While independence is admirable, refusing to involve others limits your potential. The mindset of "If I want it done right, I'll do it myself" may feel safe, but it robs you of the power of teamwork and shared creativity. This chapter will help you break free from the solo-player mindset and show you the value of building relationships, trusting others, and growing together.

Example of a Solo Player

Entrepreneur Perspective

You run your business with the mindset that no one else can also do things. You take on every responsibility—managing operations, handling customer service, and overseeing every detail—because you think, "If I delegate, it won't be done right."

When challenges arise, you tackle them alone, rarely asking for advice or input from your team or peers. While you work tirelessly, your business struggles to scale because you're stretched too thin. You don't trust others to take on meaningful roles, so growth opportunities slip through the cracks.

You're a solo player because your unwillingness to collaborate or delegate limits your business's potential. You sacrifice efficiency, innovation, and progress by trying to do everything yourself.

Working Professional Perspective

You prefer to handle projects independently, believing teamwork will only slow you down or lead to mistakes. When assigned group tasks, you quietly take over most of the responsibilities, thinking, "It's just easier if I do it myself."

While you may produce good results, your colleagues see you as someone who doesn't trust or value collaboration. You miss out on diverse perspectives and opportunities to learn from others. Over time, this solo approach limits visibility and prevents you from building strong professional relationships.

You're a solo player because focusing on working alone isolates you and stifles your growth. You miss the benefits of teamwork and collaboration by refusing to share responsibilities or ideas.

Family Perspective

In your family, you take on most of the responsibilities—planning meals, managing schedules, and making decisions—because you think, "It's quicker if I just do it myself." You rarely ask for help, feeling you must handle everything alone.

When other family members offer to assist or share their ideas, you dismiss them, believing they won't do things the way you want. Over time, you feel overwhelmed and unappreciated, while your family members feel excluded and undervalued.

You're a solo player because your reluctance to share responsibilities or involve others weakens family teamwork. By trying to do everything alone, you miss the chance to build stronger connections and foster a sense of shared effort.

Husband-Wife Perspective

In your relationship, you often take on the role of decision-maker and problem-solver. Whether managing finances, planning trips, or resolving conflicts, you handle it all yourself, thinking, "I'll just get it done faster."

While your partner wants to contribute or share responsibilities, you tend to keep them at a distance, assuming they won't do things the way you prefer. Over time, this dynamic creates frustration and imbalance—your partner feels sidelined while you feel burdened and unsupported.

You're a solo player because your desire to control everything prevents true partnership. Refusing to share responsibilities or trust your partner's input limits the collaboration and mutual support that strengthen relationships.

Core Lessons

Solo Efforts Have Limits

No matter how skilled or determined you are, you can achieve only so much alone. Collaboration allows you to reach heights you can't get on your own.

Trusting Others Multiplies Results

Delegating and collaborating unlocks others' strengths, bringing in ideas, skills, and energy that expand your impact and speed up progress.

Collaboration Builds Resilience

When you rely only on yourself, failure can feel overwhelming. Working with others provides support, encouragement, and shared problem-solving during challenges.

Signs That You're a Solo Player

In Business

You insist on handling every aspect of your business—marketing, operations, customer service—because you fear others won't meet your standards. As a result, growth stalls, and burnout sets in.

At Work

You avoid delegating tasks, even when your workload is overwhelming. You think, "If I want it done right, I'll do it myself," and hesitate to trust your team's abilities.

In Family

You take on most of the family responsibilities, from finances to household tasks, because you believe others won't do it as well or as efficiently as you can.

In Relationships

You avoid sharing your thoughts, feelings, or struggles with your partner because you believe you have to handle everything on your own. You think being vulnerable will make you seem weak.

Practical Action Steps

Identify Areas to Delegate or Collaborate

Reflect on the tasks or responsibilities that others could help with. Start with something small and allow yourself to let go of control.

Learn to Trust Gradually

Trust doesn't have to happen all at once. Give others small opportunities to prove their capabilities and build confidence in their contributions.

Acknowledge Others' Strengths

Recognise the unique skills and talents of those around you. Ask yourself, "How can their strengths complement mine?"

Ask for Help When You Need It

Practice asking for support from a colleague, family member, or partner. This builds connection and reminds you that you don't have to do it alone.

Celebrate Collaborative Wins

When you work with others and succeed, celebrate the shared achievement. This reinforces the value of teamwork.

Key Takeaways

The solo-player mindset limits growth and leads to burnout. Collaboration brings fresh ideas, shared effort, and more significant results.

Trusting others with tasks and responsibilities allows you to focus on what you do best while empowering those around you.

Working with others doesn't mean giving up control—it means leveraging strengths and building meaningful connections.

Start small, build trust, and watch how teamwork transforms what you thought was possible.

You don't have to play the game of life alone. Let others join you, share the journey, and achieve success together.

LAW 14(C)

The Law of the Team Players

"A team that trusts will never break; Stronger together with each step they take." – Farookh Sensei

Team Players

Imagine watching a group row a boat. One person rows with strength, but the ship barely moves because the others are out of sync. Now imagine that same group rowing in perfect harmony—each person matching the rhythm, pulling together toward a shared goal. The boat glides effortlessly, achieving far more as a team than anyone could.

That's the power of a team player. While individual effort is essential, teamwork amplifies what's possible. A team player knows when to lead, when to follow, and how to unite the group toward a common purpose. This chapter will teach you how to embrace collaboration, strengthen your team, and make your collective success more significant than the sum of its parts.

Example of a Team Player

Entrepreneur Perspective

As a business owner, you know the value of collaboration. You involve your team in decision-making, encourage them to share their ideas, and trust them with significant responsibilities. When challenges arise, you focus on working together to find solutions rather than trying to handle everything yourself.

You understand that you don't have all the answers and actively seek input from employees, mentors, and partners. By fostering a culture of teamwork, you not only ease your workload but also create an environment where innovation and growth thrive.

You're a team player because you recognise the strength of collaboration and empower those around you to contribute their skills and perspectives.

Working Professional Perspective

At work, you're known for being a dependable team member who values collaboration. When assigned to group projects, you actively listen to others' ideas, contribute your expertise, and help the team stay organised and focused.

You don't shy away from sharing credit for successes or stepping in to support a struggling colleague. You believe that when the team succeeds, everyone wins, and you're willing to put collective goals above individual recognition.

You're a team player because you prioritise collaboration, foster trust among colleagues, and understand that great results come from working together.

Family Perspective

In your family, you try to involve everyone in decisions and responsibilities. Whether planning a trip, organising chores, or resolving conflicts, you value each person's input and work to create a sense of shared effort.

You encourage your family to work as a team, teaching the importance of supporting one another and dividing tasks fairly. When someone is struggling, you're quick to step in and offer help, fostering an environment of trust and mutual respect.

You're a team player because you believe families function best when everyone feels included, valued, and supported in working toward common goals.

Husband-Wife Perspective

In your relationship, you see your partner as an equal teammate. You involve them in decisions, whether it's about finances, plans, or daily responsibilities. You're open to their opinions and work together to find solutions that benefit both of you.

Knowing that a balanced partnership strengthens your connection, you try to share responsibilities, from household chores to emotional labour. When challenges arise, you approach them as a team, supporting one another rather than placing blame.

You're a team player because you prioritise partnership and collaboration, ensuring your relationship is built on mutual respect, trust, and shared effort.

Core Lessons

Teamwork Multiplies Impact

When individuals work together, combining their unique strengths, they can achieve far more than anyone could.

A Team Player Supports and Inspires Others

Great team players aren't just focused on their success—they actively help others grow, contribute, and succeed.

Collaboration Requires Humility and Trust

Being a team player means valuing others' ideas, sharing credit, and trusting that everyone has a role to play.

Signs That You're Not a Team Player

In Business

You prioritise your goals over the team's objectives, resist collaboration, or dismiss others' ideas, thinking, "I can handle this better on my own."

At Work

You hesitate to share credit for successes or avoid group projects because you don't trust others to contribute effectively.

In Family

You dominate decision-making or expect others to follow your lead without considering their input or perspectives.

In Relationships

You focus on your needs without considering how decisions or actions affect your partner. You rarely ask, "How can we work together to solve this?"

Practical Action Steps

Focus on Shared Goals

Instead of asking, "What do I want to achieve?" ask, "What do we want to achieve together?" Align your efforts with the group's purpose.

Listen Actively to Others

Make a habit of seeking and valuing input from teammates, family members, or your partner. Show them that their voices matter.

Celebrate Collective Wins

Acknowledge and celebrate successes as a team, not just individually. This builds morale and strengthens bonds.

Offer Support Freely

Look for ways to help others succeed, whether offering your expertise, encouraging them, or stepping in when they struggle.

Be Open to Feedback

Accept constructive criticism with humility and use it to improve. This shows you're committed to the team's success, not just your own.

Key Takeaways

Teamwork amplifies what's possible by combining strengths, ideas, and efforts to achieve a shared goal.

A team player prioritises the group's success over individual accomplishments and actively supports others.

Listening, collaborating, and celebrating collective wins build trust, unity, and stronger teams.

Humility, trust, and the willingness to work together are the hallmarks of a true team player.

Great things are never achieved alone. Embrace the power of teamwork; together, you can reach more than you ever imagined.

LAW 15

The Law of the Perfectionists

"Perfection is slow; mistakes make you grow." – Farookh Sensei

Perfectionists

Imagine spending hours crafting the perfect email or presentation, only to delete and rewrite it a dozen times. You hesitate to share your work because it's "not ready" or "not good enough." You are caught in an endless cycle of tweaks and revisions, never feeling satisfied.

This is the struggle of the perfectionist. While aiming for excellence is admirable, perfectionism often leads to delays, burnout, and missed opportunities. Perfectionists fear mistakes, but in doing so, they fear progress itself. This chapter will help you identify the traps of perfectionism, embrace imperfection, and find freedom in taking bold, consistent action.

Example of Perfectionists

Entrepreneur Perspective

As a business owner, you have high standards for everything—your products, services, branding, and even minor details like wording emails. You spend hours perfecting things that could have been good enough to launch weeks ago.

You hesitate to release new products or ideas because they don't feel "ready." You think, "If it's not flawless, it'll hurt my reputation." Instead of testing and improving over time, you obsess over every detail before taking action. This causes delays, missed opportunities, and unnecessary stress, leaving your business struggling to grow.

You're a perfectionist because your fear of imperfection keeps you in preparation mode, preventing progress and innovation.

Working Professional Perspective

At work, you pride yourself on delivering exceptional results. But your drive for perfection means you often spend too much time on tasks, double-checking and reworking every detail. Even when a project is complete, you find flaws and wish you had more time to improve.

You avoid volunteering for new responsibilities because you worry you won't meet high standards. You think, "What if it's not perfect? I can't let people see me fail." Your need for perfection often leads to missed deadlines, overwork, and a reluctance to step out of your comfort zone.

You're a perfectionist because your unrealistic expectations prevent you from embracing progress over perfection, limiting your growth and productivity.

Family Perspective

In your family, you want everything to be just right—meals, celebrations, schedules, even the way the house looks. You spend hours planning every detail of family events, ensuring everything goes perfectly. You feel disappointed or frustrated when things don't go according to plan.

Your family often feels like they can't live up to your expectations. You hear comments like, "It's never good enough for you," or notice that they avoid helping because they feel criticised. While you want the best for your family, your perfectionism creates tension. It prevents you from enjoying the imperfect but meaningful moments.

You're a perfectionist because your need for control and flawlessness puts pressure on you and your family, overshadowing connection and spontaneity.

Husband-Wife Perspective

In your relationship, you hold yourself—and your partner— to impossibly high standards. You want your communication, routines, and even date nights to go perfectly; you feel frustrated or disappointed when they don't. You often think, "Why couldn't they do this differently?" or "This isn't how I pictured it."

You may unintentionally criticise your partner for small mistakes or things that don't align with your expectations. Over time, this creates tension and makes your partner feel like they're constantly being judged or falling short.

You're a perfectionist because your desire for an ideal relationship prevents you from appreciating the messy, imperfect moments that make love and connection authentic. By focusing on perfection, you miss the beauty of being present with your partner.

Core Lessons

Perfectionism Stalls Progress

Pursuing perfection leads to procrastination, indecision, and a fear of starting or finishing tasks. Progress, not perfection, is what drives results.

Mistakes Are Learning Opportunities

Perfectionists avoid mistakes, but mistakes are where growth happens. Every failure teaches valuable lessons that move you closer to success.

Done Is Better Than Perfect

Waiting for perfection often means never finishing. Completion allows you to learn, improve, and move forward.

Signs That You're a Perfectionist

In Business

You delay launching products, services, or strategies because they don't feel "perfect" yet. You spend excessive time on small details that don't significantly impact results.

At Work

You hesitate to share ideas or projects, fearing criticism or rejection. You spend more time polishing than progressing.

In Family

You expect everything in your household to run perfectly, from family schedules to holiday plans. You feel stressed when things don't go exactly as you envisioned.

In Relationships

You set unrealistic standards for yourself or your partner, expecting every moment to be flawless. You struggle to handle imperfections in communication or shared plans.

Practical Action Steps

Set Progress-Oriented Goals

Focus on completing tasks and making consistent progress rather than trying to achieve flawless results. Ask yourself, "What's the next step I can take now?"

Embrace "Good Enough"

Practice stopping when a task is 80% complete instead of trying to make it perfect. Often, good enough is all that's needed to achieve your goals.

Shift Your Perspective on Mistakes

View mistakes as stepping stones, not failures. After a setback, reflect on what you've learned and how you can apply it moving forward.

Set Time Limits for Tasks

Please set a deadline to finish and stick to it. This will help you focus on what matters most and prevent overanalyses.

Celebrate Small Wins

Acknowledge and reward yourself for finishing tasks, even if they aren't perfect. Completion builds momentum and confidence.

Key Takeaways

Perfectionism slows progress, creates unnecessary stress, and keeps you from achieving your goals.

Mistakes aren't failures but opportunities to learn, grow, and improve.

Progress, not perfection, is what drives meaningful results.

By setting realistic goals, embracing imperfection, and focusing on completion, you can break free from the perfectionist mindset and achieve more than ever.

The world doesn't need to be perfect—it must be done. Take the leap, finish what you start, and trust that growth comes from action, not flawless execution.

LAW 16

The Law of the Problem Solvers

"A problem solver won't turn away; They face the storm and find a way." – Farookh Sensei

Problem Solvers

Imagine being frustrated and overwhelmed in a maze because every path feels like a dead end. You keep focusing on the walls, complaining about how unfair or impossible the labyrinth is. Now imagine someone handing you a map and showing you that there's always a way out—if you're willing to step back, look at the bigger picture, and find it.

That's the mindset of a problem solver. While others dwell on the obstacles, problem solvers focus on solutions. They don't see problems as setbacks but as opportunities to learn, grow, and improve. This chapter will show you how to embrace challenges, take control of difficult situations, and turn obstacles into stepping stones for success.

Example of a Problem Solver

Entrepreneur Perspective

As a business owner, you thrive on finding solutions to challenges. When sales drop, you analyse the data to identify what went wrong. If a customer complains, you immediately investigate and work to improve their experience. You take obstacles as opportunities to refine your processes and strengthen your business.

However, sometimes, your problem-solving instinct leads you to focus on short-term fixes instead of addressing root causes. You find yourself constantly putting out fires instead of implementing long-term strategies to prevent issues from recurring.

You're a problem solver because you actively tackle challenges. Still, to maximise your impact, you need to balance quick solutions with strategic thinking for sustainable growth.

Working Professional Perspective

At work, you're the go-to person when something goes wrong. Whether it's a missed deadline, a system error, or a team conflict, you step up to resolve the issue. You take pride in your critical thinking and in providing solutions under pressure.

However, focusing on solving immediate problems often means neglecting proactive planning or delegation. You end up doing more than your share of the work, feeling like the "fixer" rather than a strategic contributor to the team.

You're a problem solver because you excel at handling crises. Still, you must step back and ensure you're addressing underlying issues and empowering others to share the load.

Family Perspective

In your family, you're the person everyone turns to when something goes wrong. Whether it's a scheduling conflict, a financial hiccup, or an emotional struggle, you're quick to step in and fix it. You pride yourself on being dependable and resourceful.

However, your constant focus on solving problems sometimes leaves little room for others to learn or contribute. You handle everything yourself, even when involving the whole family in finding a solution might be better. This can make others feel dependent or excluded from important decisions.

You're a problem solver because you're always ready to help, but to create balance, you need to encourage collaboration and share responsibilities with your family members.

Husband-Wife Perspective

Whenever your partner shares a concern or challenge, you instinctively immediately jump into "fix-it mode." You listen long enough to identify the issue, then offer a solution: "Here's what you should do," or "I'll take care of it." You want to ease their burden and show your love by being helpful.

However, sometimes your partner doesn't want a solution—they want to feel heard. Your problem-solving focus can leave them feeling dismissed or misunderstood, as though their emotions don't matter.

You're a problem solver because you're eager to help. Still, to strengthen your connection, you must balance solving problems with simply listening and offering emotional support when needed.

Focus on the Solution, Not the Problem

The more you dwell on the problem, the harder it feels to solve. Shifting your focus to potential solutions unlocks creativity and clarity.

Problems Are Opportunities for Growth

Every challenge teaches you something—about yourself, your abilities, and the systems around you. Problem solvers embrace challenges as learning moments.

Collaboration Leads to Better Solutions

Solving problems doesn't have to be a solo effort. Asking for help or seeking input from others often brings fresh perspectives and faster solutions.

Signs That You Struggle to Solve Problems Effectively

In Business

When something goes wrong, people blame external factors—competitors, the economy, or their team—rather than analysing what can be improved.

At Work

You freeze when faced with unexpected challenges, worrying more than brainstorming solutions or taking action.

In Family

You avoid addressing family conflicts or issues because they feel too complicated. You dwell on the problem but rarely take steps to resolve it.

In Relationships

You let minor issues grow into more significant conflicts because you don't address them early. You focus on what's wrong rather than how you and your partner can work together to fix it.

Practical Action Steps

Define the Problem Clearly

Please write down the problem, why it matters, and what outcome you're looking for. A clear understanding of the problem makes it easier to find solutions.

Brainstorm Solutions Without Judgment

List every possible solution, even if it seems unrealistic. The goal is to generate ideas—and sort them into outcomes later.

Focus on What You Can Control

Shift your energy toward the aspects of the problem you can influence. Ask yourself, "What actions can I take right now to improve this situation?"

Seek Input from Others

Don't hesitate to ask for advice or collaborate with others. Fresh perspectives often lead to ideas you hadn't considered.

Take Action on the Best Solution

Choose a solution and act on it. Even if it doesn't work perfectly, it provides valuable feedback for refining your approach.

Reflect and Learn

After solving the problem, reflect on the process. Ask yourself, "What worked? What didn't? What can I do better next time?"

Key Takeaways

Problems are not roadblocks but opportunities to learn, grow, and improve.

Shifting your focus from the problem to the solution unlocks creativity and progress.

Collaboration and fresh perspectives often lead to faster and better solutions.

Taking action, even imperfectly, is better than staying stuck in indecision.

Life is full of challenges, but you can face them head-on. Become the person who finds solutions, embraces growth, and turns every obstacle into an opportunity for success.

LAW 17

The Law of the Finishers

"A finisher walks where others quit; They push through doubt and never sit." – Farookh Sensei

Finishers

Imagine running a marathon and stopping 100 meters before the finish line. You've covered the distance, pushed through the challenges, and overcome obstacles—but you stop short of the goal. It's easy to start strong, but finishing requires perseverance, discipline, and a commitment to seeing things through.

The world is full of unfinished projects, abandoned ideas, and half-hearted efforts. The people who succeed are the ones who keep going when the excitement fades, and the work gets hard. This chapter is about becoming a finisher—someone who completes what they start and reaps the rewards of seeing their goals through to the end.

Example of a Finisher

Entrepreneur Perspective

As a business owner, you pride yourself on following through. When you start a project—launching a new product, redesigning your website, or streamlining operations—you ensure it gets completed, no matter what obstacles arise.

While others may abandon ideas midway, you push through challenges and setbacks, knowing that completion is what drives results. However, focusing on finishing sometimes leads to burnout, as you take on too much responsibility to see everything through.

You're a finisher because you understand the importance of completing what you start. To sustain success, you need to balance determination with delegation and self-care.

Working Professional Perspective

At work, you're known as someone who delivers. When assigned a task or project, you don't stop until it's completed to the best of your ability. You find ways to accomplish the job even when faced with tight deadlines or unforeseen challenges.

However, your determination to finish sometimes leads you to overcommit, take on extra work or refuse to ask for help. You might stay up late or sacrifice personal time to ensure nothing is left incomplete.

You're a finisher because you understand the value of follow-through. Still, you must learn to prioritise and collaborate to avoid overextending yourself.

Family Perspective

In your family, you're the one who ensures things get done. Whether organising a family trip, planning an event, or handling household repairs, you take pride in seeing things through to completion. If something starts, you make it your mission to ensure it's finished.

However, your drive to finish can sometimes leave you feeling like you're carrying the weight alone. While others might lose interest or leave tasks half-done, you push forward, even when exhausted. You sometimes wish others would step up and help carry the load.

You're a finisher because you prioritise follow-through for your family's benefit. Still, you need to encourage shared responsibility to avoid feeling overwhelmed.

Husband-Wife Perspective

In your relationship, you're the one who ensures commitments are followed through. If you and your partner make plans—like renovating the house, budgeting for a big purchase, or resolving an ongoing issue—you're determined to see them through.

However, your focus on finishing can sometimes make you impatient with your partner if they take a more relaxed or slower approach. You might feel like you're the only one pushing to get things done, which can lead to frustration or miscommunication.

You're a finisher because you understand that lasting progress comes from follow-through. Still, you must work on balancing persistence with patience and understanding your partner's pace.

Finishing Requires Focus and Discipline

Starting is exciting, but finishing requires staying focused and overcoming challenges, distractions, and setbacks.

Momentum Comes from Completion

Finishing one task builds confidence and creates the momentum to tackle bigger goals. Each win reinforces your ability to succeed.

Consistency Beats Motivation

Motivation comes and goes, but consistent effort is what drives long-term results. Finishing is about showing up even when it's hard.

Signs That You Struggle to Finish

In Business

You have multiple unfinished projects, ideas, or initiatives. You jump from one exciting opportunity to the next without fully pursuing them.

At Work

You start tasks or projects enthusiastically but lose interest or abandon them when they become tedious or challenging.

In Family

You make plans or promises—like family vacations, home improvements, or essential conversations—but don't follow through.

In Relationships

You begin efforts to improve your connection, like planning date nights or resolving conflicts, but stop before making meaningful progress.

Practical Action Steps

Set Clear Goals and Deadlines

Define what you want to accomplish and by when. Break significant goals into smaller milestones to keep yourself motivated and focused.

Track Your Progress

Use a journal, checklist, or app to track what you've completed. Seeing your progress builds momentum and reminds you how far you've come.

Push Through the Hard Parts

When the work gets tough, remind yourself why you started and focus on the result. Take a short break if needed, but don't stop altogether.

Prioritise Completion Over Perfection

Don't let perfectionism slow you down. Focus on getting things done, even if they aren't flawless. You can refine it later.

Celebrate Your Wins

Reward yourself for finishing tasks, no matter how small. Completion deserves recognition, and celebrating reinforces the habit of finishing.

Key Takeaways

Starting is important, but finishing is what transforms effort into results.

Finishing requires discipline, focus, and pushing through challenges and distractions.

Small wins create momentum and build confidence for tackling bigger goals.

Prioritise completion over perfection and celebrate your progress every step of the way.

Don't let your goals remain half-finished. Commit to the journey, see it through, and experience the success only finishers achieve.

LAW 18

The Law of the Peak Performers

"A peak performer won't stay behind; They sharpen skills and train the mind." – Farookh Sensei

Peak Performers

Imagine an athlete standing on the podium, gold medal in hand. Behind that moment of glory lies years of focused training, discipline, and a relentless commitment to excellence. Peak performers aren't just talented—they're intentional. They prioritise what matters, work smarter, and push themselves to their complete potential daily.

In life and work, peak performance isn't reserved for athletes. It's about consistently showing up at your best and striving for excellence in everything you do. This chapter will teach you the habits, mindset, and strategies to unlock your potential and operate at the highest level, no matter your field.

Example of a Peak Performer

Entrepreneur Perspective

As a business owner, you are relentless in your pursuit of excellence. You set ambitious goals, track your progress meticulously, and constantly look for ways to improve your products, services, and processes. You work long hours, invest in learning new skills, and hold yourself to the highest standards.

Your focus on being the best drives results, but it can also lead to burnout. You find it hard to slow down or delegate, believing that anything less than perfection isn't acceptable. While your business thrives, you sometimes struggle to enjoy the success you've achieved because you're always chasing the next milestone.

You're a peak performer because you push yourself to reach the highest levels of success. Still, you must find a balance to sustain your energy and well-being.

Working Professional Perspective

At work, you're the employee everyone looks up to. You consistently exceed expectations, take on challenging projects, and deliver outstanding results. You're constantly seeking improvement through training, feedback, or extra effort.

However, your drive to excel can sometimes make you overly self-critical. You rarely take time to celebrate your achievements because you're already focused on the next goal. You may unintentionally set a high standard that colleagues feel intimidated or excluded from your success.

You're a peak performer because you strive for excellence in everything you do. Still, you need to balance ambition with self-compassion and collaboration.

Family Perspective

In your family, you take pride in always going above and beyond. Whether planning the perfect holiday, ensuring the kids excel in school, or maintaining a well-organized household, you give your all to ensure your family thrives.

But your high standards can sometimes make you feel overwhelmed. You're so focused on doing everything perfectly that you rarely take time to relax or ask for help. Your family appreciates your effort but may be unable to meet your expectations.

You're a peak performer because you give your best for your family. Still, you must prioritise self-care and recognise that excellence doesn't always mean perfection.

Husband-Wife Perspective

In your relationship, you're dedicated to being your best partner. You communicate, plan meaningful moments together, and show appreciation for your partner. You work hard to create a relationship that feels fulfilling and successful.

However, your drive to be a "perfect partner" can sometimes backfire. You might overanalyse every interaction, worry about doing enough, or push for improvements when your partner wants to relax and enjoy the moment.

You're a peak performer because you're committed to building an exceptional relationship. Still, you must remember that being present and authentic is just as important as striving for excellence.

Core Lessons

Excellence Comes from Consistency, Not Talent

Peak performers don't rely solely on natural ability—they succeed because of consistent effort, discipline, and a commitment to growth.

Focus Multiplies Results

Instead of trying to do everything, peak performers focus on the tasks and goals that truly matter, cutting out distractions and unnecessary effort.

Self-Mastery Fuels Peak Performance

Managing your mindset, energy, and habits is the foundation of achieving excellence. Peak performers invest in themselves before anything else.

Signs That You're Not Operating at Peak Performance

In Business

You spend your time juggling too many tasks or goals, often feeling busy but unproductive. You avoid refining your priorities or systems to maximise efficiency.

At Work

You do just enough to meet expectations but rarely push yourself to exceed them. You procrastinate developing skills or taking on challenges that could advance your career.

In Family

You show up for your family but often feel distracted, overwhelmed, or inconsistent in your efforts to connect or support them meaningfully.

In Relationships

You let minor misunderstandings fester, avoid deep conversations, or neglect intentional efforts to grow the connection with your partner.

Practical Action Steps to Become a Peak Performer

Set Clear, Measurable Goals

Define what peak performance means for you in specific terms. Break your big goals into smaller, actionable steps to track progress.

Prioritise What Matters Most

Focus on the tasks, relationships, or projects that align with your values and have the highest impact. Learn to say no to distractions or low-priority activities.

Create Daily Rituals for Success

Develop habits that fuel your performance, like starting your day with clear intentions, regular exercise, and consistent learning.

Invest in Your Energy

Peak performers understand that rest and recovery are as important as hard work. Maintain balance by getting enough sleep, eating well, and managing stress.

Embrace Growth Over Comfort

Push yourself beyond your comfort zone regularly. Whether taking on a challenging project or learning a new skill, growth comes from discomfort.

Reflect and Adjust

Review your progress regularly, identify what's working and what isn't, and refine your strategies to keep improving.

Key Takeaways

Peak performance is achieved through consistency, focus, and self-mastery, not talent or luck.

Prioritising the most impactful tasks and eliminating distractions amplifies results.

Rest, recovery, and balance are essential for sustaining peak performance over time.

Growth happens when you challenge yourself and consistently aim for excellence, not perfection.

Every day is an opportunity to show up as the best version of yourself. Commit to peak performance, and watch as you unlock your full potential, one step at a time.

LAW 19

The Law of the Mentors/Coaches

"A coach won't stop, they won't step back; They drive you forward, keep you on track." – Farookh Sensei

Mentors & Coaches

Think back to when someone believed in you before you believed in yourself. Maybe it was a teacher, a manager, or even a friend. They didn't just tell you what to do—they asked questions, shared wisdom, and helped you see possibilities you hadn't considered. That's the power of a coach or mentor.

Mentorship isn't about control or authority—it's about creating a space where growth flourishes. Whether you're guiding others or seeking guidance, a great mentor shapes lives, unlocks potential, and leaves a lasting legacy. In this chapter, you'll learn the principles of effective coaching and mentoring and how they can create ripple effects of growth in others and yourself.

Example of a Mentor/Coach

Entrepreneur Perspective

As a business owner, you take pride in helping others grow. You mentor your team by sharing the knowledge and experience you've gained over the years. Whether it's coaching an employee on leadership skills, guiding them through challenges, or encouraging them to take on more prominent roles, you prioritise their growth alongside the success of your business.

However, sometimes, you struggle to balance guiding and micromanaging. You might feel frustrated when your team doesn't immediately adopt your advice or when they make mistakes. Learning to empower them without taking over has been a key growth area for you as a leader.

You're a mentor because you understand that investing in others' development creates a stronger, more capable team. By fostering their growth, you're also ensuring the long-term success of your business.

Working Professional Perspective

At work, you're the person colleagues come to for advice or guidance. You enjoy sharing your expertise, whether helping a new hire learn the ropes or offering feedback to a struggling teammate. You take pride in seeing others succeed and often step into informal leadership roles to support your team.

However, your willingness to help can sometimes lead to overextending yourself. You may spend so much time mentoring others that you neglect your tasks or professional development. You're working to balance supporting others and focusing on your growth.

You're a mentor because you prioritise helping others achieve their potential. In doing so, you build stronger relationships and a more collaborative workplace.

Family Perspective

In your family, you naturally take on the role of guide and teacher. Whether it's helping your children navigate challenges, teaching life skills, or offering advice to siblings, you're always there to support their growth. You celebrate their successes and encourage them to learn from their mistakes, fostering resilience and confidence.

At times, your role as a mentor can make you overly involved. You might find it hard to let family members figure things out independently, or you might feel unappreciated when your efforts go unnoticed. Learning to step back and trust them to apply what they've learned is essential to your growth as a family mentor.

You're a mentor because you're committed to guiding your family toward becoming their best selves while strengthening the bonds between you.

Husband-Wife Perspective

In your relationship, you often act as a source of support and guidance for your partner. Whether they face career challenges, personal struggles, or big decisions, you're there to listen, offer advice, and encourage them to keep moving forward. You believe in their potential and take pride in helping them grow.

However, your mentoring instinct can sometimes lead you to offer solutions when your partner wants emotional support. They may feel you're trying to "fix" them rather than simply being there for them. Balancing advice with empathy and understanding has been critical in deepening your connection.

You're a mentor because you care deeply about your partner's growth and success. By thoughtfully offering guidance and encouragement, you strengthen your relationship and build a foundation of trust and mutual respect.

Core Lessons

Mentorship Multiplies Growth

A mentor isn't just a teacher—they're a multiplier. By guiding others, they amplify knowledge, skills, and confidence, creating results far better than one person could achieve alone.

Empathy and Active Listening Are Key

A great mentor listens more than they speak. They seek to understand the needs, goals, and challenges of those they guide, offering advice tailored to the person, not just the situation.

Mentorship Is a Two-Way Street

While the mentee grows from the mentor's guidance, the mentor also learns, evolves, and gains new perspectives through the relationship.

Signs That You're Not Fully Embracing Mentorship

In Business

You struggle to delegate tasks or develop your team because you feel doing things yourself is faster. You rarely invest time in training or guiding others.

At Work

You hesitate to seek advice from experienced colleagues or avoid mentoring juniors, thinking it's "not your responsibility."

In Family

You focus more on solving problems for your family members than teaching them how to handle challenges themselves.

In Relationships

You offer advice to your partner without first understanding their perspective or helping them come to conclusions.

Action Steps to Embrace the Role of a Coach/Mentor

Start by Listening

Whether you're mentoring someone at work, in your family, or in a relationship, focus on understanding their goals and challenges. Ask open-ended questions like, "What's most important to you now?"

Share Experiences, Not Just Advice

Instead of telling someone what to do, share relevant stories from your life. Show how you handled similar situations, including the mistakes you made and the lessons you learned.

Encourage Self-Discovery

Ask guiding questions to help the other person arrive at their solutions. For example, "What options have you considered?" or "What do you think could work best?"

Provide Constructive Feedback

Be honest and specific when giving feedback, but always frame it in a way that inspires growth. Instead of saying, "This isn't good enough," say, "Here's how this could be even better."

Be Consistent and Supportive

Outstanding mentorship isn't a one-time conversation. Commit to regular check-ins and be available for support, encouragement, and guidance.

Seek a Mentor Yourself

Just as you guide others, make it a priority to find someone who can mentor you—learning from those who have walked the path before you is invaluable.

Key Takeaways

Great mentors multiply growth by guiding others to discover their strengths, solve problems, and achieve their goals.

Empathy, active listening, and asking thoughtful questions are the foundation of impactful mentorship.

Mentorship is a two-way relationship where the mentor and the mentee grow, evolve, and gain valuable insights.

Commit to being a consistent, supportive presence in others' lives while seeking mentorship to continue your growth.

A great coach or mentor doesn't just teach—they inspire. By empowering others, you leave a legacy that grows far beyond yourself. Start guiding, learning, and watching how

mentorship changes lives—including yours.

LAW 20

The Law of the Good Leaders

"A good leader listens, a good leader learns; Respect is something a leader earns." – Farookh Sensei

Good Leaders

Imagine a captain steering a ship through a storm. The crew is anxious, the waves are high, and the destination feels far away. A good leader doesn't shout orders from a safe cabin—they stand with their crew, guiding them calmly, earning their trust, and showing them the way forward.

Leadership isn't about authority or titles but service, connection, and improving those around you. Good leaders don't just focus on results; they focus on people. This chapter will teach you the principles of good leadership and how to lead with integrity, empathy, and purpose, whether in your business, workplace, family, or relationships.

Example of a Good Leader

Entrepreneur Perspective

As a business owner, you strive to lead with integrity and purpose. You prioritise your team's growth and well-being, ensuring they feel valued and supported. You communicate your vision, set achievable goals, and inspire others to work toward a common purpose.

You make it a point to listen to your team's concerns and ideas, fostering an environment where they feel safe contributing. When challenges arise, you don't blame others—you focus on finding solutions and leading by example. Your leadership builds trust, motivates your team, and creates a strong foundation for long-term success.

You're a good leader because you empower your team, lead with empathy, and focus on creating an environment where everyone thrives together.

Working Professional Perspective

At work, you're seen as someone who naturally takes on leadership roles, even if you don't have an official title. You guide your team by providing direction, staying calm under pressure, and setting a positive example. You're approachable and try to listen to your colleagues' perspectives, ensuring everyone feels heard.

When your team succeeds, you share the credit. When there's a setback, you take responsibility and help others learn from the experience. You inspire confidence by staying consistent, honest, and reliable, which motivates your peers to trust and follow your lead.

You're a good leader because you focus on collaboration, accountability, and creating a culture of respect and trust within your team.

Family Perspective

In your family, you lead by example, showing kindness, patience, and responsibility. You guide your family through challenges with a steady hand, encouraging open communication and ensuring everyone feels supported. You involve family members in decisions, helping them feel valued and included.

When conflicts arise, you focus on resolving them fairly and calmly, setting the tone for a respectful and harmonious household. You make time for family bonding and ensure that everyone understands the importance of working together as a team.

You're a good leader because you create a nurturing environment where your family can grow, connect, and overcome challenges.

Husband-Wife Perspective

In your relationship, you approach challenges with patience and understanding, setting the tone for healthy communication and problem-solving. You support your partner's goals and dreams, offering encouragement and stepping in to share responsibilities when needed. You lead by being consistent and dependable, showing that your actions align with your words.

You listen to your partner's concerns and needs, ensuring they feel valued and respected. When decisions need to be made, you collaborate, ensuring the outcome reflects your perspectives. Your leadership creates balance, trust, and a sense of unity in your relationship.

You're a good leader because you prioritise partnership, empathy, and mutual respect, ensuring your relationship is built on a strong and supportive foundation.

Core Lessons

Good Leadership Is Rooted in Service

The best leaders prioritise the needs of their team, helping others grow, succeed, and thrive. Leadership is about lifting others, not standing above them.

Trust Is the Foundation of Leadership

Good leaders build trust through transparency, honesty, and consistency. Without trust, leadership becomes control, and control doesn't inspire loyalty.

Empathy and Communication Drive Connection

Understanding the emotions, goals, and challenges of those you lead fosters deeper connections and better teamwork. Leaders who listen inspire engagement and commitment.

Signs That You're Struggling with Leadership

In Business

You focus solely on metrics and results, neglecting your team's well-being, growth, and morale. You notice disengagement but don't address it.

At Work

You avoid taking responsibility for team setbacks and hesitate to provide support or guidance when colleagues need help.

In Family

You prioritise control over collaboration in family decisions, leaving others feeling unheard or undervalued.

In Relationships

You focus on "leading" the relationship by making decisions unilaterally instead of working as a team to understand your partner's needs and goals.

Practical Action Steps

Lead by Example

Demonstrate the qualities you want to see in others. Be honest, hardworking, and consistent in your actions. People follow what they see, not just what they hear.

Practice Active Listening

Create space for open communication. Ask for feedback, listen without interrupting, and show that you value others' perspectives.

Prioritise People Over Outcomes

Focus on building relationships and fostering a positive environment. When people feel supported and valued, they perform better.

Be Transparent and Honest

Share your vision, goals, and challenges openly. Transparency builds trust and makes others feel included in the journey.

Recognise and Celebrate Contributions

Recognise the efforts and successes of those you lead regularly. Gratitude boosts morale and motivates people to continue giving their best.

Invest in Others' Growth

Encourage learning, provide resources, and mentor your team members or family. A good leader helps others reach their potential.

Key Takeaways

Good leadership is rooted in service, trust, and empathy. It's about guiding and lifting others, not controlling them.

Building strong connections through communication and active listening creates an engaged, motivated, and loyal team.

A good leader leads by example, practices transparency, and celebrates the contributions of others.

Authentic leadership isn't about personal success but your impact on those you lead.

Becoming a good leader isn't about perfection—it's about progress. Lead with integrity, inspire trust, and watch your leadership transform others and yourself.

LAW 21

The Law of the Great Leaders

"A great leader knows success won't last; Unless they help the torch be passed." – Farookh Sensei

Great Leaders

Imagine a leader who achieves goals and leaves a lasting legacy. Their team isn't just motivated—they're transformed. They don't just inspire results—they inspire others to lead.

Outstanding leadership goes beyond managing tasks or guiding people—it's about creating a powerful vision that aligns with everyone's strengths and inspires them to go beyond what they thought was possible. Great leaders build trust, empower others, and foster a culture of excellence. This chapter will help you uncover the qualities of a great leader and teach you how to elevate your leadership to leave an impact that lasts a lifetime.

Example of a Great Leader

Entrepreneur Perspective

As a business owner, you're not just focused on running your company—you're driven by a vision that inspires those around you. You lead purposefully, clearly communicating the bigger picture and ensuring every team member feels connected to that vision. You empower others by delegating responsibilities, trusting their abilities, and encouraging innovation.

When challenges arise, you maintain composure and guide your team with resilience and optimism. You don't just focus on profits—you prioritise creating a positive culture, investing in people, and making a lasting impact in your industry and community.

You're a great leader because you inspire action, build trust, and elevate everyone around you, leaving a legacy of growth and excellence.

Working Professional Perspective

At work, you're more than just a high performer—you're the person who inspires your colleagues to rise to their potential. You don't seek recognition for yourself; instead, you lift others by mentoring, encouraging collaboration, and creating opportunities for shared success.

You focus on the bigger picture, ensuring your team's goals align with the organisation's mission. When things get tough, you remain calm, make thoughtful decisions, and motivate others to persevere. You're approachable, empathetic, and always willing to listen, creating an environment where others feel safe to innovate and grow.

You're a great leader because you lead with humility, inspire confidence, and create a workplace culture that brings out the best in everyone.

Family Perspective

In your family, you don't just guide your loved ones through daily routines—you lead with intention and vision. You set the tone for open communication, ensuring everyone feels heard and valued. You teach by example, demonstrating the importance of kindness, resilience, and responsibility.

You focus on building a legacy of love and connection, helping your family establish traditions, values, and goals that bring them closer together. Even during difficult times, you lead gracefully and optimistically, showing your family that challenges can be overcome when you work together.

You're a great leader because you prioritise unity, inspire growth, and leave a lasting impact on your family by fostering a culture of trust, love, and mutual support.

Husband-Wife Perspective

You lead with purpose and commitment, ensuring your partnership is built on trust, respect, and shared vision. You're proactive in addressing challenges, working with your partner to find solutions that strengthen your bond. You're not just focused on day-to-day tasks—you think about the bigger picture, helping achieve your personal and shared dreams.

You inspire your partner by being emotionally present, empathetic, and supportive of their growth. You lead by example, demonstrating resilience, kindness, and humility in every interaction. You create a safe space for your partner to thrive, encouraging them to reach their potential while building a future together.

You're a great leader because you lead with love, understanding, and a vision for a thriving, fulfilling relationship that inspires you and your partner to grow together.

Core Lessons

Vision Is the Heart of Great Leadership

A great leader has a clear vision that inspires and aligns people. They communicate this vision passionately, making others believe in the possibilities ahead.

Empowering Others Creates Legacy

Great leaders don't hoard power—they give it away. They develop leaders, empower teams, and create an environment where others can thrive and grow.

Great Leaders Act with Integrity and Purpose

Leadership isn't just about results but how you achieve them. Acting with authenticity, empathy, and purpose builds trust and respect.

Signs That You're Not Operating as a Great Leader Yet

In Business

You focus primarily on achieving short-term goals and managing tasks. Still, you haven't created a long-term vision that inspires your team to dream bigger.

At Work

You handle your responsibilities well but rarely mentor or develop others to take on leadership roles.

In Family

You lead by setting rules and expectations, but don't create a shared family vision or empower others to contribute equally to the family's growth.

In Relationships

You focus on solving problems or meeting day-to-day needs but don't work with your partner to build a shared vision for the future or inspire mutual growth.

Practical Action Steps

Define and Communicate Your Vision

Take time to clarify your long-term goals and the "why" behind them. Share this vision with your team, family, or partner in a way that inspires them to join you in achieving it.

Empower Others to Lead

Identify strengths in those around you and mentor them to step into leadership roles. Create opportunities for them to take ownership and contribute.

Lead with Integrity

Make decisions that align with your values and purpose. Consistency and authenticity in your actions build trust and respect from those you lead.

Encourage Collaboration and Innovation

Foster an environment where everyone feels valued, heard, and free to share ideas. Collaboration breeds creativity and strengthens the team.

Focus on Long-Term Impact

Think beyond immediate goals. Ask yourself, "What legacy do I want to leave behind?" Let this guide your leadership decisions.

Celebrate and Share Success

Give credit where it's due, highlighting the efforts of others. Great leaders recognise that their success is built on the contributions of the people around them.

Key Takeaways

Great leadership is about vision, empowerment, and integrity. It's not just about guiding people—it's about inspiring them to reach their full potential.

A great leader focuses on long-term impact, creating a legacy by empowering others to lead and grow.

Building trust, fostering collaboration, and acting purposefully are the cornerstones of transformational leadership.

True greatness isn't about individual success—it's about leaving a positive, lasting impact on those you lead.

Great leaders inspire, empower, and elevate. Step into greatness by creating a vision worth following and a legacy worth remembering.